LOST PHOTOGRAPHS OF THE RNLI

LOST PHOTOGRAPHS OF THE RNLI

EDWARD WAKE-WALKER

Lifeboats

SUTTON PUBLISHING

For all those remarkable individuals
I have met at stations around the coast,
most of them volunteers, who launch, man,
administer and raise money for the lifeboats.

First published in the United Kingdom in 2004 by
Sutton Publishing Limited · Phoenix Mill
Thrupp · Stroud · Gloucestershire · GL5 2BU

British Library Cataloguing in Publication Data
A catalogue record for this book is available from the British Library.

ISBN 0-7509-3718-1

Typeset in 10/14pt Sabon.
Typesetting and origination by
Sutton Publishing Limited.
Printed and bound in England by
J.H. Haynes & Co. Ltd, Sparkford.

Contents

Acknowledgements

I am indebted to Charles Campbell, not only for bringing the lost photographs back to the RNLI, but for the invaluable information he provided about Amos Burg and his extraordinary life.

I have also been very kindly treated by a number of my former colleagues at RNLI headquarters and in the divisional bases who have made the job of researching this book easy and enjoyable. Particular thanks go to Derek King for his help with photographs, Barry Cox for ensuring fruitful library sessions, Janet Smith for tracking down some essential information, Hugh Fogarty for casting a seasoned mariner's eye over the text and David Brann and his team in the Fundraising and Communications department for their practical support of the project.

Officials and crews of lifeboat stations featured in this book have given me the warmest of welcomes and willing assistance on my fact-finding travels round the coast and I am extremely grateful to them. I should also like to thank Tony Ellis of Humber Coastguard for his help in providing details about the Life Saving Appliance volunteers who feature so prominently in the book. Thanks also go to both Simon Stevens of the National Maritime Museum and model shipwright, Malcolm Darch, for valuable information on ships and to Alastair Brown for his encouragement as my mentor in the world of post-RNLI self-employment.

Finally, I must acknowledge my family's contribution: Fiona, who encouraged me to persist in my search for a publisher and who accompanied me through the sand-dunes to Sker Point on the wettest and windiest of Welsh November afternoons; Thomas, who was always on stand-by to rectify my crises with the computer, and Eleanor, an occasional sounding-board, of whose help with Chapter 20 only she and I will ever know the true value.

Map showing the locations of the events in this book

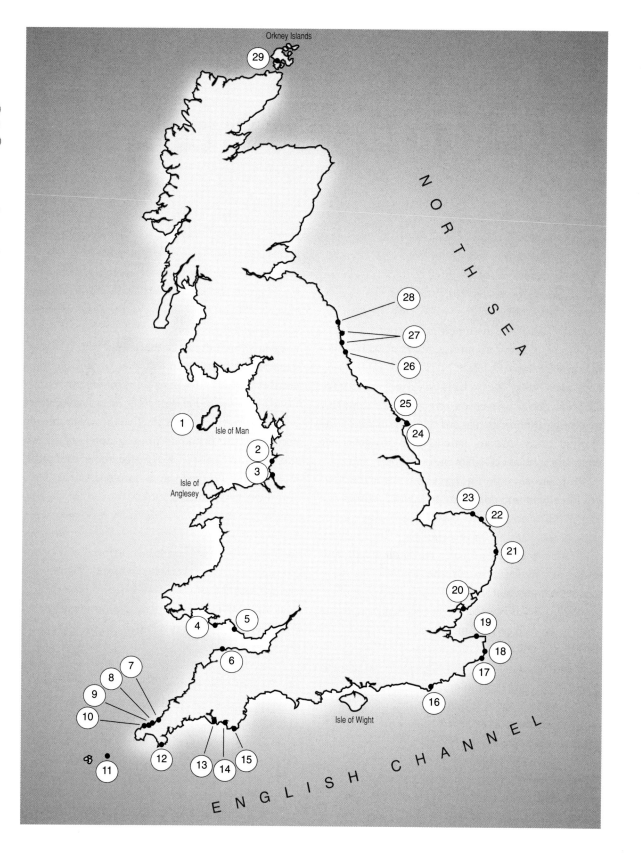

Introduction

A scene exists in my imagination which takes place back in 1948 in the public relations office of RNLI headquarters at 42 Grosvenor Gardens, London SW1. The publicity secretary, Charles Vince, has just returned from his lunch and is being told by his young assistant about a gentleman who called in and who had just left.

'You did what?' he exclaims, aghast. 'Surely I have told you that we never, on any account, let people take original photographs out of this building? If he wanted prints for an article, you should order copies for him, not give him the originals!'

'But he was going back to America and couldn't wait for copies to be made,' comes the reply. 'He also said his publishers couldn't use copies, they had to have originals. The *National Geographic* magazine has very high standards, you see. Anyway, I'm sure he'll return them, he was a very pleasant man.'

'Well, I doubt we shall ever see them again and from what you've told me, they were some of the best in our collection.'

Assuming such an exchange took place, Mr Vince was right; neither he nor his assistant would ever see those originals again. They did not know, however, that more than half a century later, all thirty-seven photographs would find their way back to RNLI headquarters, now in Poole, Dorset, personally delivered to the public relations director of the day by a resident of Juneau, Alaska, who had come across them in a shack on the shores of the Gastineau Channel.

More can be discovered in the first chapter of this book about Amos Burg, the man who borrowed – but seemingly never published – the pictures, and about Charles Campbell, their rescuer. I am only sorry that neither Burg nor the supposed PR assistant will ever know that their combined administrative peccadilloes have been instrumental in bringing about a book which celebrates both the era they lived through and the return of the precious photographs. With any luck, they will also have caused some additional, if somewhat delayed, funds to come to the RNLI through the sale of the book.

These photographs, their light hidden under a bushel for so many years, deserve to be published now and the stories behind them told. One can only guess at the criteria for their selection by Amos Burg on his flying visit to London, but he was himself an accomplished photographer for the *National Geographic*, so he knew what made a good picture.

It is an unusual task, however, to write a book based entirely upon someone else's chosen illustrations. What would make the incidents they depict hang together? Some lifeboat stations such as St Ives and Cromer seem to get more than their fair share of attention at the expense of other equally distinguished outposts of the RNLI. Some of the featured events, particularly the tragedies,

Padstow's pulling and sailing lifeboat, *Arab*, rounding Stepper Point in a gale. She was stationed there between 1883 and 1900.

were unquestionably turning points for the lifeboat service and helped to mould its future. Others, however intriguing, would normally have soaked back into the fabric of the Institution, sometimes remembered by a paragraph in *The Lifeboat* journal or a single line on a service board in a lifeboat station, but generally forgotten.

It was immensely rewarding, therefore, to retrieve the detail that lay behind the sketchy captions scrawled on the back of the photographs. Like those tight shells children used to drop into a glass of water and which would spring open to reveal bright, re-hydrated flowers, my research among old newspapers has brought characters, their adventures and misadventures vividly back to life.

What gives all these stories a coherence is that together they shed light on one of the most formative fifty-year periods in the long and illustrious history of the Royal National Lifeboat Institution. They start at the turn of the twentieth century, when the only chance of survival for a shipwrecked crew still rested on the grim determination of ten men at the oars of a pulling lifeboat, or a rocket line fired from the shore.

They take us through the days of the first motorised lifeboats, when crews' early mistrust of mechanisation was soon replaced by enthusiastic and expert deployment.

We see Robert Smith of Tynemouth steaming 45 miles down the north-east coast in a gale to rescue 130 people from a wrecked hospital ship. Henry Blogg of Cromer drives his motor lifeboat right on to the deck of a stranded barge to take off her man and boy, and Tommy Cocking of St Ives manoeuvres deftly between a cliff and a stricken steamer to bring her crew to safety. Each was achieving feats unthinkable aboard pulling lifeboats and demonstrating to an increasingly wide and admiring public a new and apparently limitless capability.

Some might even argue that motor lifeboats encouraged coxswains and crews to push themselves too far. Should the ill-fated St Ives lifeboat have put out, pitting her slight 6-ton weight against one of the worst Atlantic storms in living memory, to answer a vague distress signal from a ship 11 miles away? At what point did the single engine aboard The Mumbles lifeboat cease to provide enough control to William Gammon as he closed in on the *Samtampa*?

Though disastrous and tragic, both these missions at least served to remind the world that the sea could never be conquered, however brave and skilful its adversary. Perhaps they helped to relieve the pressure of public expectation of dramatic success felt by every coxswain as he set out on a rescue. Certainly, the era of these photographs was one in which the lifeboatman's fan club began to spread rapidly inland thanks to increasing mass communication.

Many of the pictures featured were in the vanguard of photo-journalism, finding their way into both local and national newspapers. Rescuers and survivors were invited by the BBC to broadcast their experiences to the nation. Thanks to the likes of Pathé News, Henry Blogg became almost as much of a household name as Rudolph Valentino or Jesse Owens.

It was also a time when large numbers of people began to take seaside holidays and took home with them memories of visits to the lifeboathouse and meetings with strong, silent crewmen. Children, parents and grandparents were indelibly affected by the ethos of the volunteer lifesaver and it is fair to say that even today, the RNLI benefits through gifts and legacies from individuals whose first images of the lifeboat service were similar to those in this book.

These pictures also allow us to remember another group of stout volunteers, the often unsung lifesaving appliance companies, ready with their rocket lines and ladders, to pluck survivors ashore, directly from their wrecked ships. Until the ship-to-shore breeches buoy rescue was eventually superseded by the helicopter winch wire, some nineteen-thousand individuals were saved by these men. By coincidence, the last story of the book records the first joint lifeboat and helicopter mission, thus heralding the next giant leap forward in sea rescue after the advent of the motorised lifeboat.

We are allowed a glimpse, too, of how women played an important role in sea rescue long before the first female lifeboat crew members were enlisted in the 1970s. The no-nonsense launchers on the Northumberland coast reveal the true resilience of the female spirit, especially in small communities where every able-bodied human being had their part to play when the lifeboat was needed.

Other revolutions in technology, in addition to the internal combustion engine, had a marked effect on the lifeboat service in the first half of the twentieth century. The period begins when communication between lifeboat and shore is confined to signal flags and flares; it ends with some lifeboats fitted with radio telephones and the era of radar and radio direction finding not far away.

Man had not yet flown when the Ilfracombe lifeboat launched to the stranded *Aberlemno* in 1897. By 1930 the RNLI introduced a uniquely fast lifeboat at Dover, specifically designed to speed to any aircraft, among the growing number carrying passengers between London and the Continent, that might come down in the Channel. Barely a decade later, during the Second World War, it was aircraft, either by dint of their own destruction or due to the damage they inflicted on others, that were a principal cause for the crews of the RNLI being called out more often than at any previous time in the Institution's history.

There are a number of wartime rescues featured in this book. At the time they took place, much of the detailed information about the incidents remained unpublished for fear of helping the enemy in some way. The return of these photographs means that at last there is an opportunity to pay tribute, through a few examples, to the remarkable bravery of crews who had a human as well as an elemental enemy to face when they put out on a rescue mission.

Above all, though, what the incidents in this book show us is that whatever period you choose to focus on out of the 180-year story of the lifeboat service, you find the same thing: ordinary people going to extraordinary and selfless lengths to save the lives of others. The following extract from an unforgettable paean to a lifeboat (see Chapter 6), happily remains as true today as it was when Winston Churchill delivered it back in 1924:

> It drives on with a courage which is stronger than the storm, it drives on with a mercy which does not quail in the presence of death, it drives on as a proof, a symbol, a testimony, that man is created in the image of God, and that valour and virtue have not perished in the British race.

Today the Royal National Lifeboat Institution is a thriving organisation, still largely dependent on volunteer crews to man its 231 lifeboat stations

The Tyne class lifeboat, *David Robinson,* at sea out from the Lizard where she has been on station since 1988. (*Courtesy of the Royal Bank of Scotland/Rick Tomlinson*)

carries out widespread work to prevent accidents on the water, and many amateur sailors have benefited over the past ten years from its water safety advice, freely offered in pamphlets, videos and lectures.

The annual cost of running this vital national emergency service, extending to the furthest corners of the British Isles, is approximately £100 million a year. What many people find astonishing is that every penny is paid for each year through voluntary contributions and legacies. Apart from a very brief period in the middle of the nineteenth century, the taxpayer has never been asked to contribute to the lifeboat service in all its 180-year history.

Supporters of the RNLI, its crews and the armies of volunteer fundraisers have always valued the independence that non-reliance on the state has afforded them and there is every intention to keep it that way in the future. It means, of course, that people must continue to provide for the charity through voluntary gifts, subscriptions, membership and a mention in their will. This book chronicles an era which helped to mould the RNLI of today and to make it a rescue service which is the envy of the world. Any reader wishing to become a supporter and to help guarantee success in the next sixty years of this remarkable service should contact the RNLI at West Quay Road, Poole, Dorset, BH15 1HZ (Tel. 01202 663000) or visit the website at www.lifeboats.org.uk.

on the coast of the United Kingdom and the Republic of Ireland. Every year crews are called out more than 7,000 times and more than 7,000 people have reason to thank them for their rescue.

Modern lifeboats range in size from the 17-metre 25-knot all-weather Severn class to the 4.9-metre D class inflatable, invaluable for inshore work. Recently the RNLI also introduced rescue hovercraft into its fleet, which have enabled crews to reach casualties on previously inaccessible areas for lifeboats, such as mud flats and sandbanks.

The RNLI can now also be seen operating on holiday beaches, predominantly in the south-west of England, providing a lifeguard service. It also

WHERE TO FIND THE 'LOST' PHOTOGRAPHS

Additional images from the RNLI photo collection and other sources have been used further to illustrate the stories behind the original thirty-seven 'lost' photographs returned from Alaska. The 'lost' photographs themselves appear on the following pages: 8, 12, 16, 20, 22, 23, 26, 30, 36, 42, 48, 54, 58, 62, 66, 72, 76, 78, 80, 82 (top), 84, 90, 96, 100, 106, 112, 118, 122, 126, 134, 140, 144, 148, 152, 156, 162, 168. Unless otherwise stated all photographs are the property of the RNLI. Enquiries about obtaining copies of photographs in this book should be directed to the RNLI Photo Library at the above address.

1 The Two Americans

Who Lost and Found the Photographs

CHARLES CAMPBELL – THE FINDER OF THE PHOTOGRAPHS

When Charles Campbell and his wife Ellen arrived, unannounced, at the headquarters of the RNLI in Poole, Dorset, on 3 October 2002, carrying the package which they had nursed so tenderly on their long journey from their home in Juneau, Alaska, they began to wonder what sort of reception awaited them. They might have drawn some encouragement from a display in the reception area depicting important moments in the history of the lifeboat service; at least this overtly twenty-first century organisation had some appreciation of its past. Their journey was going to be pretty pointless if it did not.

Campbell, originally from Virginia and an official of the federal prison service, moved to Alaska in 1979 when he became the state's Director of Corrections. After his retirement, he built a house in Juneau on the banks of the Gastineau Channel and in 1998 acquired his neighbour's house when it came on to the market. It had previously belonged to one Amos Burg, a man

whom Campbell had much admired and whose widow, Carolyn, eventually sold him the house. Burg had settled there when he finally married at the age of fifty-seven, after an extraordinary life of travel and adventure which had taken him to some of the remotest corners of the world.

What Charles Campbell had not bargained for when he bought the house was that two of its outbuildings down on the beach were still stacked high with thousands of documents, photographs, logs, notes, cuttings and other memorabilia, compiled and collected by Amos Burg in the course of his eventful life. No one had touched them since Burg had died twelve years previously and now, as the owner of the property, Campbell realised that if he didn't sort, clear and archive the material, no one else would.

It must have been almost as daunting an undertaking as one of Burg's own wild canoe trips through the wildernesses of North America, but the discoveries Campbell made among the minutiae amassed during such a restless life were

Charles Campbell, the man who found the lost photographs in Juneau, Alaska and returned them to the RNLI.

his reward. Among those discoveries was an envelope containing a few dozen, mainly 10in × 8in black and white photographs which, unusually for Burg, had no accompanying note to explain how he had come by them.

Unlike most of the photographs in the two sheds, these were not prints of Burg's own work; instead they were a varied collection of scenes spanning a fifty-year period and crediting journalistic agencies from all parts of the United Kingdom. Apart from their salt-water subject matter, they only had one thing in common: stamped on the reverse of every one were the words: 'Please return to the Royal National Lifeboat Institution, 42 Grosvenor Gardens, London SW1'. As far as Campbell could discern, the earliest picture had been taken in 1897, the latest in 1948.

With the conscience of a true archivist, Charles Campbell resolved that these historic photographs, clearly only on loan, should be returned to their rightful UK home before they were once again forgotten. This was the mission on which he and his wife were bound when they tentatively explained to the receptionist at the RNLI's Dorset head office that they had a package to hand over to someone involved with heritage matters. They were both enormously relieved to discover just how much the return of the photographs was appreciated at the RNLI. Missing original images of a proud era of the Institution's history had been restored, immeasurably enhancing the visual archive at a stroke.

It will never be known for certain how or why the photographs came into Amos Burg's possession, but a look at the life of this remarkable man will explain why he would have been so interested in the work of the lifeboat crews of the United Kingdom and Ireland.

AMOS BURG – EXPLORER, ADVENTURER, PHOTOGRAPHER, FILM-MAKER AND JOURNALIST (1901–86)

Born in 1901 of a Norwegian father, Burg spent his boyhood in the wilds of the West Coast state of Oregon, wandering along the sloughs and lakes of the Columbia River, fishing for sunfish and catfish. Very early on he discovered in himself a longing to know what lay round the next bend in the river to the east and an equal impatience to see with his own eyes the mysterious lands he had been told lay beyond the Pacific horizon to the west.

His parents understood his wanderlust enough to allow him, still aged only fifteen, to spend his summer vacation working as bell-boy aboard a passenger ship which ran between his home town of Portland, San Francisco and Los Angeles. Although he did return to school in the autumn, the experience at sea had cast an indelible spell on him. He spent his time in the school library gazing, he recalls, 'at colored pictures of the South Seas with their surf-lined coral islands, waving coconut palms and laughing, carefree, brown-skinned natives'.

By January, he had abandoned high school and was off in search of the real thing. It was relatively simple in 1918 for an American teenager to persuade a ship's captain to take them on as an untrained junior hand. Burg made his first crossing of the Pacific that year to Sydney via Hawaii, Pango Pango and Samoa. By the end of that year, he had returned home, set off again immediately aboard a small, wooden coal-burning steamer to sail round the world, weathered ferocious winter storms in the northern Pacific, been promoted to able seaman, witnessed a mutiny by members of the crew in Shanghai and survived the attentions of a knife-wielding Japanese cook.

His circumnavigation was completed in June the following year in spite of a fire in the engine room off Hong Kong and a sand-storm in the Red Sea. His next trip was almost his last; on a ship carrying timber to Manchester, he was swept off the deck by a huge wave in darkness off the Irish coast. As he went over the side, he caught a lifeline and was eventually able to haul himself back on board. Then, setting off from Antwerp on his return to the United States, his ship was rammed by another steamer and badly damaged. Small wonder, perhaps, that the existence of a lifeboat service in the waters of the British Isles was of such interest to Amos Burg later in his life.

It was in 1920, during a break between voyages, that Burg made his first serious canoe trip into the hinterland of North America. He and a shipmate, neither with any experience of negotiating rapids, rode the Snake and Columbia

Amos Burg, who continued to explore the coastline of Alaska late into his seventies.

Rivers from Lewiston, Idaho, to the Pacific in a 16ft craft. Several times they only narrowly escaped disaster.

By now, Burg was beginning to realise that his urge to travel was fired not so much by the business of getting to destinations across vast oceans; rather it was the landscapes and the peoples he encountered when he arrived which fascinated him. When he went to sea, he always took with him two trunks, one for clothes and personal items, the other for the complete 24-volume set of the *Encyclopaedia Britannica*. He spent all his spare time at sea immersed in its pages, desperate not to waste his waking hours and ravenously accumulating knowledge about foreign countries, their people and their animals.

When his ship reached port, he would observe his fellow sailors with understanding as they set off on a spree of wine and women to alleviate shipboard monotony. For him, though, a new destination was a new opportunity to visit street markets, museums and zoos which would bring vividly to life what he had been reading about in the pages of the encyclopaedia. He also realised there was extra money to be made buying up oriental goods such as silks, pearls and rugs and selling them on his return home.

The longer Burg spent away from America, the more his beloved *Britannica* would lie open at the pages which told him about the great rivers of the USA and Canada. Inspired by early explorers such as Lewis and Clark, his thirst to emulate them grew and grew. Now in his early twenties, he spent the next few years undertaking increasingly perilous and arduous canoe expeditions, interspersed with the study of journalism and photography at university.

In 1922, paddling his canoe single-handedly, Burg covered a phenomenal 4,000 miles in 135 days, travelling from Livingston, Montana, the headwaters of the Yellowstone River to New Orleans and the Gulf of Mexico via the Missouri and the Mississippi. Then, in October 1924, in spite of an injured knee, snow and ice, he embarked on the 1,200-mile descent of the Columbia River, from its source in Canada to the Pacific. Using newspaper to insulate his legs and body, he crossed the river bar into the Pacific the following January, the first man ever to complete the trip.

That remarkable feat made him famous in his home town of Portland, where he was given banquets and honours and asked to speak at noon luncheons. He was soon off again into the wilds, however, this time to tackle the entire length of the Snake River, through Wyoming and Idaho, then into the Columbia River and to the sea. The trip cost him both his treasured canoe, *Song O' the Winds*, which was wrecked in the Grand Canyon of the Snake River and also his dignity, if not nearly his life, when he capsized in front of Fox Movietone and International Newsreel cameramen near his home town of Portland. He was carried 2 miles downstream in the icy water before he managed to struggle ashore.

After another trip to China to supply his import business and two further canoe trips (one through the Inside Passage along the coast of Alaska, the other, a second full descent of the Columbia), Burg had his first big break as a cameraman and journalist. He was asked by an Oregon newsreel producer to travel north to film the annual caribou migration across the Yukon River in Alaska. The *National Geographic* was also keen to publish an article about the voyage. This trip, together with his next adventure, helped to establish Amos Burg as a nationally renowned explorer, photographer and film-maker.

Bizarrely, on what would be his most northerly and potentially gruelling expedition, Burg chose to take as his travelling companion an ageing doctor of philosophy, George Rebec, from the University of Oregon, a man who had never camped out a day in his life and who had a bad heart. The purpose of the trip was to canoe north through Alberta up the Athabasca and Slave Rivers, through the Great Slave Lake and then 500 miles further north up the Mackenzie River and out into the Arctic Ocean. Burg records that he had to do all the paddling while the professor sat in the stern of the canoe 'spilling out the knowledge he had accumulated through nearly three-quarters of a century'.

Far from being driven to distraction, Burg clearly appreciated every moment of his marathon lecture. It was only when the two men had covered three-quarters of their journey that he finally managed to persuade the protesting academic – by now showing signs of pneumonia –

to abandon the canoe and take a steamboat back to civilisation.

During his return from this epic voyage, Burg was wired an invitation to address 4,000 members of the National Geographic Society in the Washington Auditorium, Washington, DC, about his earlier trip to the Yukon. It was the first of many lectures he would give to impressively large and learned audiences throughout the USA. The year was now 1930 and he was increasingly in demand for filming assignments, but that year he also found time to make two further canoe trips: the entire length of the Columbia River (again) and the entire Snake and Columbia descent (again).

In 1931 the *National Geographic* sent him on a round-the-world trip aboard a 225ft luxury yacht. It took him from the Caribbean, through the Panama Canal and across the Pacific to French Indo-China via Tahiti, Fiji, the Solomon Islands, New Guinea, Bali, the Philippines, Saigon and many other exotic staging posts. The voyage continued via Singapore, Sumatra, Ceylon, Aden, Suez and Rhodes to Istanbul where Burg caught the Orient Express to Paris. He returned home, crossing the Atlantic aboard the liner *Majestic*, where he was afforded a suite to himself. It must have been a peculiar contrast to his more accustomed mode of travel, perched on the thwart of a canoe.

It did not take long for him to return to more familiar surroundings. After surviving a charge by a bear while filming on Admiralty Island in Alaska, he started to plan an expedition to the southern extremity of the American continents. Finally forsaking his canoe, he shipped out a 25ft, ex-US coastguard surf boat in which he and a companion negotiated the Strait of Magellan and explored the archipelagos which surround Tierra del Fuego. In all, they encountered thirteen gales, one of which blew at hurricane strength for five whole days.

They spent two months living and filming among the Yaghan people who were on the verge of extinction, hitched a ride around Cape Horn aboard a three-masted barque and then voyaged some 1,000 miles north through the Patagonian channels to Puerto Montt on the Chilean coast.

By way of contrast, Burg sailed to England in April 1937 to cover the coronation of George VI. As he stood on a platform in front of Buckingham Palace, he remembered being close to tears as he photographed all the units of the British Empire as they processed past him: the famous British regiments, the Canadian Mounties, the Bengal Lancers, Australians, South Africans and even one representative from the island of the *Bounty* mutineers, Pitcairn. As they marched off into the distance, he felt that he had seen 'the marvellous sights and sounds of a great democratic empire dying away forever'.

After the coronation he launched his ever-handy canoe into the Thames and paddled from London to Liverpool via the Grand Union, Birmingham Navigations and Shropshire Union canals. Even though it meant hand-cranking 400 locks, it must still have seemed like a Sunday outing compared with his usual canoeing exploits. His article about this trip was published three years later in the August 1940 issue of the *National Geographic* under the title, 'Britain Just Before the Storm'. It painted an idyllic picture of rural England, but again with a sense of a final glimpse of something splendid, never to be experienced again.

In 1938 Burg completed what he described as 'one of the most awe-inspiring and dangerous river voyages in the world'. He and Haldane 'Buzz' Holstrom became only the thirteenth expedition to navigate the canyons of the Green and Colorado Rivers since John Wesley Powell's historic journey in 1869. The idea was to make a film re-creating the first-ever single-handed navigation which Holstrom had accomplished the year before. Each man had his own boat, Holstrom using the wooden boat he had built for his lone voyage and Burg becoming the first man to use an inflatable rubber boat on the river. They completed the 1,300-mile trip in seventy days, having passed through eighteen great canyons which lie between the Green River lakes in Wyoming and the Hoover Dam on the borders of Nevada and Arizona. Burg's film of the expedition, which he sold to 20th Century Fox, was nominated for an Academy Award in 1939.

It was around this time that Amos Burg became the owner of a 36ft converted US coastguard lifeboat, *Endeavour*, which he bought from the man who had captained the very first ship in which Burg had sailed at the age of fifteen. He was to own the boat for more than forty years, often living aboard her for several months at a time and taking her on long explorations up the west coast of North America to Alaska. The boat, which had left coastguard service in 1928, was of a design directly derived from the lifeboats of the RNLI and therefore a contemporary 'first cousin' to many of the boats which feature in the rescue stories told in these pages. This was surely another reason why Burg made his postwar visit to RNLI headquarters to borrow some photographs.

Before America entered the war, Burg found himself on some nerve-racking filming assignments in the Far East. He was in Japan in 1940 during the war between Japan and China and under frequent suspicion of spying. He was, in fact, extremely fond of the Japanese and was mortified, therefore, when the attack came on Pearl Harbor in 1941. Before that, while making another film deep in the heart of China, he had his own experience of Japanese bombing, surviving twenty-one devastating air raids on the city of Chung King.

In 1943 Burg was recruited on a special assignment by the US government, spending several months in the southern regions of Argentina and Chile. Presumably his knowledge of the area was useful, although his only comment on what he described as his 'James Bond activities' was that misrepresenting himself and the need for secrecy gave him indigestion.

His next filming trip in the countries of Central America gave him dysentery but that was more than compensated for by the knowledge that, for the first time, he was working for Encyclopaedia Britannica Films. At last he was able to add some of his own knowledge to the publication which had inspired and fed his own passion for discovery.

Burg came to Britain to make films in 1947, 1948 and 1949. He claimed his most nightmarish experience was filming down a coal mine in Scotland, crawling hundreds of feet in a 24in seam, thousands of feet underground. The following year's assignments sounded more pleasant, beginning in Spain in 'the little village of Torremolinos', then flying to London and travelling to York for a film about English children. If a Nona Hodgson, who featured as a little girl in the film, should ever read this book, she may be pleased to be reminded of the deep regard in which Amos Burg held her and her family ever since.

It would appear that 1949 was the last time Burg came to Europe, travelling via England to Bergen in Norway, finally tracking down his roots and filming in his father's homeland. There is no record of whether it was on his return from this trip or the previous one that he stopped off at the RNLI headquarters. Whichever year it was, the photographs he borrowed were destined to remain on the north-west coast of America for more than half a century, perhaps cruising aboard the old US lifeboat *Endeavour*, in the company of twenty-four volumes of *Encyclopaedia Britannica* for at least some of that time.

The iron barque, *Aberlemno*, high and dry in Ilfracombe's outer harbour, waiting for repair after her grounding.

8

2 Aground in a Blizzard

Aberlemno, an iron barque, off Ilfracombe, 2 April 1897

The fact that it was three thirty in the morning when the coastguards' signal sounded to summon the lifeboat did nothing to curb the concern and curiosity of the Ilfracombe locals who hurried in their scores to the slipway to find out what mishap that night's foul weather had caused.

When they arrived at the harbour, most found that the lifeboat, the 37ft, twelve-oared *Co-operator No. 2*, was already away and the crew pulling hard at the oars, eastwards along the coast towards Watermouth and Sampson's Caves. The word was that a large vessel had gone aground there, some time just after midnight. With that information, people began to drift back home again, knowing there was not much they could do or see, at least for the next few hours.

Some stayed at the harbour-side to await further news. When it arrived, it was a shock to many of them. The ship in distress was the *Aberlemno*, owned by Alderman Morgan Tutton; she was one of the famous Swansea copper-ore-men, a familiar sight in the Bristol Channel for many years. What was more, her skipper was Captain T. Birmingham, a well-known Ilfracombe man, much

appreciated for his genial manner about the town. This was, in fact, Captain Birmingham's first voyage in the *Aberlemno* and it had been fraught with difficulties from the start. A full month had passed since he and his crew of fifteen hands embarked from Glasgow, their ship laden with 1,170 tons of house coal destined for Buenos Aires. The barque's progress along the Firth of Clyde was soon halted by adverse weather and for six days the ship had been forced to lay off just under Greenock.

When at last she resumed her voyage, she made good progress down through the Irish Sea and had almost reached as far south as Land's End when, on St Patrick's Day, she was hit by a tremendous squall. The captain decided he should seek shelter immediately and turned the ship round and ran before the gale up the Bristol Channel to the safety of the Penarth roads. There they stayed, weather-bound, for a fortnight. Then, on the afternoon of 1 April, the *Aberlemno* attempted for a third time to wrestle her way clear of British waters and head south towards Argentina.

The weather was still not particularly favourable with sleet and rain in the morning, but in the afternoon it seemed to clear. A steamboat took the barque in tow and cast her off in the Bristol Channel when she was clear of land. The wind was light but by 6 p.m. it had strengthened and veered round to the north-west. Just under two hours later they passed the Break Sea lightship and the weather was clear.

The mate of the *Aberlemno*, James Alexander, speaking to the reporter of the *Ilfracombe Chronicle* after the event, remembers being called on deck some four hours later just as a heavy squall struck the ship. Immediately she became enveloped in a blinding storm of snow and dense fog. The mate was shocked to hear the tell-tale sound of breakers close by and just as he was giving orders to put the helm hard down, there was a ghastly shudder as the hull struck solid rock.

There was consternation on board as to how the ship could be so much off course, the popular view later being that there was a deflection of the compass. Immediately distress signals were lit, men went below to look for signs of water ingress and the captain considered strategies to save the ship.

Mercifully for Captain Birmingham, an alert coastguard had seen his signals. The nearest village to them was Combe Martin and the first

people to reach the ship after the alarm was raised were men from this village. They succeeded in getting on board and, with the cooperation of the *Aberlemno*'s crew, began making strenuous attempts to haul the barque off the rocks.

When the Ilfracombe lifeboat arrived on the scene, her crew drenched by fierce wintry squalls and constant spray from the rough seas, the ship was still hard aground. They used the lifeboat to lay out a kedge anchor and her men then lent their weight with the others on the windlass aboard the *Aberlemno* and, inch by inch, she was coaxed off the rocks.

At first her captain thought he would sail her straight back across the Bristol Channel to Penarth for repairs, but he soon realised that he had too large a hole in the bottom of his ship and with 3ft 6in of water slopping around inside her already, he needed to find safety closer to hand.

For the people of Ilfracombe it made a very pretty sight to see the *Aberlemno* running into the outer harbour under full sail at about 9 a.m. that same morning, especially when they knew that their lifeboat crew had been instrumental in saving her. Her captain, however, would doubtless have chosen any harbour in the world

Ilfracombe pulling and sailing lifeboat, *Co-Operator No. 2*, returning to station after an exercise.

Above: The town turns out for a ceremonial launching of *Co-operator No. 2*.
Right: Ilfracombe harbour.

other than his home town to leave a vessel, high and dry, waiting ignominiously for repair after an accident that had occurred under his command.

The *Aberlemno*, already more than twenty years old at the time of this mishap, went on to serve Alderman Tutton for eight years before she was sold into Norwegian ownership in 1905 and rechristened *Durban*. In 1917 she was fired upon by a German submarine to the west of Ireland while on passage between Cuba and Copenhagen. Although substantially damaged, she escaped her attacker and made harbour. She was repaired the following year, at the same time being fitted with two 69hp Skandia engines. Renamed *Mary* by her new Swedish owners in 1920, she was finally broken up in 1923.

3 The Boxing Day Hurricane

Plymouth, 26 December 1912

Three men, leaning on a wall which overlooked the Sound, ducked their heads in perfect synchronisation as a large sheet of corrugated iron flew clean over them, missing them by a hair's breadth and landing on the beach below. It turned out to be part of the roof of the Ladies' Bathing Place, one of the many properties in Plymouth and the surrounding area to suffer damage in the violent storm that hurtled into the West Country on Boxing Day 1912.

On her way to the public wash-houses in Hoegate Street, Mrs A. Cooksley, aged seventy, of New Street, was blown clean off her feet as she rounded the corner at the top of Hoe Street and was later found to have fractured and dislocated her shoulder. William Drake, a fisherman of Commercial Road, was walking along Sutton Road when a quantity of wooden hoarding was hurled across the street, burying him beneath it. Rescuers found him alive but with a broken leg. Fortunately, no one was standing near a large glass case containing hats

and other items, hung outside Mr Stephens's milliner's shop in Tavistock Road, when it crashed to the ground.

Elsewhere, roof-slates flew through the air, chimneys collapsed into upper-storey rooms and trees were uprooted. At Totnes Castle several elms fell, destroying part of a stable and coach-house. A four-wheeled trap was wrecked, but luckily the horse escaped unscathed.

With such turmoil on land it was small wonder that much worse things were happening at sea. It had been a stormy period leading up to Christmas and shipping in the Channel was proving a precarious and time-consuming business. The schooners *Ottawa* and *Guild Mayor* and the Newport-based ketch, *Johnny Toole*, had been especially hampered in their trade. All three ships had been weather-bound in Portland a few days earlier, and, after a brief resumption of their voyage, once again found themselves seeking refuge from the wind and sea, this time in Plymouth Sound.

The continual delays were particularly frustrating for the crew of the *Johnny Toole* who had left Cowes

Opposite: Devastation in Plymouth Sound: from left to right, the dismasted *Guild Mayor*; the *Ottawa*; Plymouth lifeboat, *Eliza Avins*, temporarily aground, her crew awaiting the flood tide; and the river steamer *Goyaz*.

three weeks earlier with a cargo of cement for Salcombe and who, on reaching their destination, had found the harbour bar too dangerous to cross, forcing them to sail on to Plymouth for shelter. Her skipper chose an anchorage inside the Cattewater where a number of other ships were also taking refuge. Here, the skipper's wife was taken on board, so at least one man in the crew would spend Christmas with family.

The two schooners still had long voyages ahead of them. The three-masted, 230-ton *Ottawa*, with her five-man crew, was taking manure from London to Waterford. The two-masted *Guild Mayor* was bound from Poole for Runcorn with a hold full of china clay. Their captains let go their anchors further out in the Sound, near its eastern shore at Jennycliff. They were close to another vessel which must have attracted their crews' interest for a while. She was a brand new twin-funnelled river-steamer, the *Goyaz*, built in Holland and destined for Para in Brazil. Her very shallow draft and high super-structure, ideal for the rivers of Brazil, were not cut out for winter sea-borne passages and she and her Dutch crew had been holed up in Plymouth since October, waiting for calmer conditions.

It was two in the morning when the big storm broke. By seven the tide was at its height and the breakwater therefore offered the least protection from the huge seas stampeding into the Sound before the southerly gale. By nine hurricane-force gusts of 83mph were being recorded and every crew of every ship riding at anchor knew that before long something would have to give.

The men on board the *Guild Mayor* were already aware that their ship had dragged her anchor closer to the shore. Then, to their horror, they saw that the *Goyaz*'s cable had parted and the steamer was bearing straight down on them, her high side acting like a sail before the wind. There was no escape; within seconds the two

vessels came together with an agonising sound of creaking and cracking timber. With the impact, the bowsprit, foremast and main topmast of the *Guild Mayor* were wrenched from their footing and crashed over the side.

The rampaging *Goyaz* then shrugged herself clear of the debris alongside the schooner and continued like some deranged somnambulist towards the rocky shore. There she sat, remarkably level, on a ledge of rock, increasingly high and dry as the tide receded. Her crew were able to walk ashore.

By a miracle, no one was badly hurt aboard the schooner and although she was, in fact, to remain afloat throughout the storm, her crew all scrambled into the ship's lifeboat and made land by running alongside the steamer and clambering over her.

The following day, the mate of the three-masted *Ottawa*, Mr W. Roberts, gave an account of his experience to a reporter of the *Western Morning News*:

> Early yesterday morning it came on dirty and we had two anchors down. The wind veered to the westward but about 9am the starboard anchor chain parted and the vessel began to drag. The crew hastily bent a spare anchor on what was left of the starboard chain but no sooner was this let go than it again parted and the port anchor proved insufficient to hold the schooner. We drifted into Batten Bay and the vessel was very soon on the rocks although we did everything to save her.

The men of the *Ottawa* were not alone in their attempt to save their ship and themselves. The tug, *Boarhunt*, was out in the Sound and, at considerable risk, had once got near enough to the *Ottawa* to pass a line aboard while she was still afloat. Unfortunately, the crew did not have time to make the line fast before the two vessels moved apart and the schooner hit the rocks.

Meanwhile, the Mount Batten Apparatus Lifesaving Brigade had made their way across the rocks and boarded the stranded *Goyaz* to get as near as they could to the point where the *Ottawa* had come ashore. And, of course, the Plymouth lifeboat, the ten-oared *Eliza Avins*, was out. Her crew had never seen seas so large in Plymouth Sound. Somehow they got alongside the *Ottawa* when they saw she was aground. They attached a line to the schooner and as some men fought to hold the two craft side by side, others man-handled the crew aboard the lifeboat. It was a perilous and lengthy process and all the time the tide was ebbing, bringing the lifeboat's keel closer and closer to the rocks beneath. At last they were able to pull away from the side but the men at the oars could not make any headway against the wind and sea. It was all that they could do to keep the lifeboat's head to sea and for a whole hour they were battling simply to keep clear of the rocks.

When the battle finally proved to be in vain and the lifeboat first bumped and then settled more firmly on the bottom, the coxswain knew that all he could do was to wait until the tide turned and refloated him. It was freezing cold and his crew were exhausted, but it was his only option. The five survivors, however, had other plans. They could see that four members of the Lifesaving Brigade had courageously swum a short distance of boiling sea between the *Goyaz* and some rocks close to the lifeboat to see what help they could give. Against the coxswain's advice, the five men left the lifeboat and struggled through the shallows and were grabbed by the lifesaving men on the rocks. Soaking wet, they nevertheless reached warmth and comfort sooner than the lifeboat crew who waited stoically with their boat until it refloated, more or less unscathed.

By now, the *Johnny Toole* was also a casualty in the Cattewater. As the storm had gathered in the early hours, the ketch's anchor had begun to drag. In spite of dropping a

Mount Batten as it appears in 2004. (*Edward Wake-Walker*)

second anchor, she was soon ashore on Queen Anne's Battery Point. The captain, his wife, the mate and a single crew member got ashore without mishap, although, in an effort with the tugs *Mildred* and *Reindeer* to tow her off, a sudden squall sent her back aground in an even worse position on a rocky ledge.

Now leaking badly, she looked to be a total loss. However, she was later salvaged and repaired, only to fall victim to a German submarine in the First World War. The *Guild Mayor* was also towed to safety as the storm subsided and the *Goyaz*, aground for several weeks, eventually came off the rocks and was repaired and made it to Brazil.

4 The First 'Light' Motor Lifeboat

Named at Eastbourne, 27 September 1922

According to a mildly irreverent account in the *Eastbourne Chronicle*, the moment depicted in this photograph when the Bishop of Lewes, the Right Revd Dr Southwell, prayed that the town's new lifeboat 'by God's gracious help and ready presence, might be the means of saving many lives', had come not a moment too soon for the thousands gathered under the Wish Tower for the occasion. The bishop's dedication promised that the end of the handing over and naming ceremony was finally in sight. The crowd had already endured an hour of speeches and the unreliable weather threatened a downpour at any moment. The *Chronicle* explained:

The speeches were certainly informative and well worth listening to under more favourable circumstances, but the vast majority of the crowd were too far off to hear what was said, and naturally enough became somewhat impatient to see the important part of the event, namely the launch.

This desire found expression in a long outburst of applause, the humour of which, we trust, was kindly regarded by the worthy gentleman who chanced to be addressing the gathering at the time.

The speechmakers can, perhaps, have been forgiven a little for getting carried away by the occasion as it marked a very important milestone in the RNLI's development and also a centenary for Eastbourne lifeboat station. The lifeboat receiving her name was the first, capable of being launched from a carriage or a shelving beach, to be fitted with an engine. Until that time, the size of motorised lifeboats limited them to slipway stations and afloat moorings. Now a much smaller, lighter design had been tested and approved, and this heralded the eventual phasing out of pulling and sailing lifeboats.

The boat in question was the self-righting, 35ft RNLB *Priscilla Macbean*. She was named after the wife of Edward Macbean, a Glasgow manufacturer of oilskin clothing whose legacy

Opposite: The Bishop of Lewes blesses the new, motorised Eastbourne lifeboat before her naming and official launch.

17

to the RNLI had provided the £10,000 needed to build her. Her total weight was less than 6 tons and her 15hp engine, referred to as an auxiliary, gave her a speed of 6 knots and a radius of action of 80 miles. She had a crew of eight and, at a pinch, could accommodate fifty survivors.

The Eastbourne crew had been given plenty of time to lose any lingering attachment to a pulling boat with the first launch of the motor lifeboat taking place the previous December. According to the district inspector of lifeboats, Lieutenant F.W. Hayes RNR, in his speech at the ceremony, conditions at that time were the worst she was ever likely to encounter. The night was dark, the tide was low, a full gale was blowing and a very heavy sea running. Apparently the lifeboat behaved in such a way as to gain the complete confidence of the Institution, the officers at Eastbourne and of her crew. Be that as it may, it did not stop one of the longer-serving crew members complaining that the new boat had made him feel seasick for the first time in his career.

He might have felt it earlier had it not been for the First World War. That was the message (for those who could hear), from the Hon. George Colville of the RNLI Committee of Management as he officially handed the lifeboat over to the station. Because of the war, the lifeboat had taken a long time to build and was five years overdue. The war had, in fact, held up the RNLI's entire modernisation scheme which made the Institution appear to be rather well off at that time.

He assured the fundraisers present that the impression of considerable assets was false and that the money had long been earmarked to be spent on new motor lifeboats all around the coast. Scarborough would be the next place to receive the new carriage-launched motor lifeboat and with only 37 of the RNLI's 238 stations equipped with motorised boats, there was a lot of building and expenditure planned. The annual cost of running the RNLI had, in fact, reached £300,000 but Mr Colville was at pains to point out that they were providing excellent value for money and that the state-run lifeboat service in the USA cost proportionately twice as much. As more of the reserves were being spent on modern lifeboats, the Institution was earning less through investment income and so he congratulated the Eastbourne Ladies' Lifeboat Guild on their latest annual flag day total of £583, a great effort in the face of the current acute trade depression.

When the Mayor got up to speak, he seized on a claim made earlier by the acting station chairman that Eastbourne was the oldest lifeboat station on the coast and this, he felt, 'bears out what I have often said: Eastbourne leads and others follow'. In fact, he had himself been misled. At least twenty-one stations predated Eastbourne, including its near neighbour, Newhaven, established in 1803.*

No one, however, would have begrudged him his show of civic pride that day. The town had supported a lifeboat station since 1822, two years before the RNLI itself was founded. Her crews had saved eighty-eight lives in those 100 years. Before him, ready to launch, was the groundbreaking new motor lifeboat dressed overall with bunting and with her coxswain, Henry Boniface, and crew standing erect in the stern. Behind the speakers' platform was the station's old pulling and sailing lifeboat, *James Stevens No. 6*, still used as a back-up, equally

---

* The two oldest lifeboat stations, still operating today, are Sunderland, Tyne and Wear, and Montrose, Tayside, both established in 1800.

bedecked with flags and serving as a platform for the All Saints Church choir. The town band were arrayed in front of the William Terriss Memorial Lifeboat house,* smartly clad VIP guests surrounded the dais and citizens of Eastbourne thronged the neighbouring parade and the grassy slopes leading up to the Wish Tower.

A huge cheer rose when, finally, Mrs Astley Roberts, President of the Eastbourne Ladies' Guild, named the lifeboat *Priscilla Macbean*, released the champagne and, to the strains of 'Rule Britannia', the lifeboat, her propeller turning, accelerated down the beach and into the sea.

The old pulling and sailing lifeboat, *James Stevens No. 6*, kept as a back-up to the new motor lifeboat. The William Terriss Memorial Lifeboat house can be seen in the background. (*Courtesy of Graham Farr*)

* So named because it was funded by an appeal run by the *Daily Telegraph* in memory of the Victorian actor-manager and Adelphi Theatre owner, William Terriss, who was murdered in 1897. Richard Prince, a 'resting' actor, held a grudge against Terriss for sacking him for unprofessional behaviour and heavy drinking. Wrongly believing Terriss was refusing him grants from the Actors' Benevolent Fund, Prince set upon him as he entered a side door of the Adelphi and stabbed him three times with a dagger. The lifeboat house is now used as a museum, raising tens of thousands of pounds every year for the RNLI.

The current Eastbourne lifeboat, *Royal Thames*, a Mersey class, seen here exercising off Beachy Head. (*Royal Bank of Scotland/Rick Tomlinson*)

5 Victims of the Weather off the Lizard

Adolf Vinnen and *Nivelle*, February and June 1923

There is a ship's bell on display in the Top House, the southernmost pub on the British mainland, whose landlord is the current operations manager of the Lizard lifeboat station. The bell once hung aboard the *Adolf Vinnen*, a 1,525-ton German sailing ship and will always remind local people of the part their village played in the rescue of her crew on a wild February night in 1923. When the *Nivelle* ran aground in fog four months later, she left Lizard inhabitants an altogether more incendiary reminder of her misfortune.

The year had seen one of the stormiest Februaries on record with more than fifty RNLI lifeboats in action and close on forty lives saved by their crews. In the late afternoon of Friday the 9th, the wind, which had been blowing hard from the south for some time, increased to gale force and huge waves began to thunder against the rocky cliffs of the Lizard.

In the failing light, from the shore a sailing ship with five towering masts could be seen, apparently in some difficulty as she battled westward in mountainous breaking seas. The vessel was the brand new *Adolf Vinnen*, launched only three months earlier in Kiel and on her maiden voyage to Barry Dock in South Wales to take on a cargo of coal. Despite the additional aid of two powerful diesel engines, she found herself being driven closer and closer to the shore. Soon the men on duty at the Lloyds signal station on Bass Point realised, helplessly, that this great ship would run aground on the rocks of Green Lane Cove, almost directly beneath their station.

Even before she struck, the Lizard lifeboat had launched from her slipway in Polpeor Cove and

Previous spread, right and opposite: Daylight reveals the hopelessness of the *Adolf Vinnen*'s plight. Her crew are hauled to safety by breeches buoy.

22

the rocket lifesaving team was trundling equipment across the fields towards the casualty. Coxswain Richard Stephens at the helm of the 38ft motor lifeboat, *Frederick H. Pilley*, had a tremendous job on his hands just to maintain a course eastward to reach the schooner as massive seas bore down on his starboard side. It took half an hour to travel barely a mile. The neighbouring Cadgwith lifeboat, the pulling and sailing *Minnie Moon*, had also launched but was forced back to her station after failing to make any headway whatsoever in the weather.

When the lifeboat crew eventually caught sight of the ship, she was lying broadside on to the shore, about 70yds from the cliffs, her decks repeatedly enveloped by the ferocious breaking seas. The lifeboat let go an anchor and veered down towards the *Adolf Vinnen*. Her crew got a grapnel on board but in the strong tide that was running, the lifeboat was in great danger. One of her crew told a reporter later:

> We saw from the first that there was no hope for the barque. We tried to get alongside but found it quite impossible owing to the mountainous seas. At one moment we would be on the crest of a wave and the next down in the trough with the seas towering above us. In our attempts to get alongside we were on two occasions nearly hurled on board the barque.

For more than an hour the lifeboat's coxswain persevered but no one on the ship showed any inclination to come on board. Then he saw that

the Lifesaving Appliance Brigade had successfully landed a line across the ship and the captain was shouting at him to pull clear out of danger.

Once Richard Stephens had seen that the breeches buoy was successfully rigged and that members of her 24-man crew were being hauled ashore, he turned the lifeboat and headed north-east for Falmouth. It would have been suicidal to try to land the lifeboat back at Polpeor on the southern tip of the Lizard so the only alternative was a long, fearsome passage past The Manacles to Falmouth. The coxswain later said that it was the worst experience he had ever been through. In the pitch darkness, the lifeboat was twice filled with heavy seas and both times he had to call the roll to check that none of his men had gone overboard.

They reached Falmouth at midnight, soaked to the skin, freezing cold and utterly exhausted. Looked after by the local lifeboat branch for the night, they awoke next morning to be met with the astonishing news that seven men aboard the *Adolf Vinnen*, including the captain, had refused to leave the ship and had spent the night in the rigging. Immediately, the Lizard lifeboat set out once more to see what help could be given.

It was a huge relief to the rescuers on the cliff-top when, as dawn came, the *Adolf Vinnen*'s captain, accepting at last the hopelessness of his ship's plight, signalled that they would now like to come ashore. It was not a moment too soon for any of the seven men, especially the chief officer who had damaged his ribs in a fall by the engineroom during the night. The operation (shown in the accompanying photographs), took 35 minutes to complete, the captain being the last to leave the ship. It was all over before the lifeboat could get there and she returned once more to Falmouth, as it was still too rough to make it back to Polpeor.

Although he had lost his brand new ship, the German skipper was still generous in his praise of the skill and courage of the lifeboat crew. He said:

Opposite: Exhausted but alive: two crewmen from the *Adolf Vinnen* on the cliffs above their wrecked ship.

The Lizard's 38ft motor lifeboat, *Frederick H. Pilley*. (Courtesy of Graham Farr)

Your lifeboat was handled in a masterly manner and I was afraid she would be dropped on our deck or smashed against our side, so I ordered her off. I did not wish the brave fellows to further imperil their lives.

The early summer of the same year brought another difficult job for the crew of the Lizard lifeboat. This time the culprit was dense fog which clung stubbornly to the Cornish coast on the night of Saturday 9 June. It came in with a strong south-westerly wind that made for rough conditions as the steamer *Nivelle* rounded Land's End and set a course up the English Channel. The ship was owned by the Normandy Shipping Company of London, her skipper and crew were Sunderland men and she was carrying coal from Newport to Rouen.

Captain Joseph Brown knew the Lizard was near at hand as he peered into the thick, black night, hoping to see the reassuring glimmer of the Lizard light over his port bow, telling him he was clear of land. No sign came; instead, just after

Opposite: The steamer, *Nivelle*, aground in Pentreath Bay.

27

midnight on Sunday the 10th, the *Nivelle*'s progress came to a shuddering halt as her bow met the rocks at the foot of the cliffs of Pentreath Bay, just a mile to the north of Lizard Head.

The current immediately swung the steamer's stern to the north so that she lay parallel to the shore, her bow among rocks and her stern resting on the sandy beach. The forepeak began to fill with water and a nasty bulge appeared in her side. The captain radioed for help and was relieved to receive an almost instant response from the Lizard Lighthouse. All he knew was that he was aground somewhere to the west of the Lizard and three lifeboats were therefore called to try to find him. Penlee lifeboat, stationed on the far side of Mount's Bay, was launched but had to turn back almost immediately with engine trouble. The pulling and sailing lifeboat at Porthleven also put out but returned to station having found nothing.

Meanwhile, the crew of the Lizard lifeboat, *Frederick H. Pilley*, hugging the rocky western shore of the peninsula, soon came upon the ghostly form of the *Nivelle*, looming out of the fog, the surf crashing against her side. Then they saw that one of the ship's boats had been launched; it was cruising around to seaward of the wreck, unable to make it ashore in the heavy surf.

The captain had ordered the ship to be abandoned when the rising tide reached the level of the steamer's rail and the entire crew of twenty had clambered into one boat. By the time the lifeboat drew alongside, the overloaded boat was full of water and it was with huge relief that the men climbed into the lifeboat. It was a further three hours before the lifeboat could be safely beached back at her station and the survivors put ashore.

Unlike the *Adolf Vinnen*, the *Nivelle* lived to fight another day. Refloating her entailed offloading her cargo of coal on to the beach. With an understandable abhorrence of waste, local inhabitants were quickly on the scene, salvaging what would otherwise have been claimed by the sea. But when this free supply of fuel was put to use in Cornish ranges, owners were in for a shock. Their ranges were burnt out in the heat, for this was not domestic coal but Grade 1 steam coal for locomotives. No one had told them that.

The Lizard lifeboat station at Polpeor.

Above: Pentreath Cove at low tide. (*Edward Wake-Walker*)

Left: The modern Lizard lifeboat sets out from her station at Kilcobben. (*Royal Bank of Scotland/Rick Tomlinson*)

Below: The boiler and other wreckage from the steam trawler *Maud* is still visible today at low tide. She came to grief in February 1912 in an identical position to the *Nivelle*'s grounding. (*Edward Wake-Walker*)

Robert 'Scraper' Smith, Tynemouth lifeboat coxswain from 1910 to 1920. He held one Gold and two Silver RNLI bravery medals.

6 Robert 'Scraper' Smith of Tynemouth

Centenary Guest of Honour in London, 2 July 1924

For Coxswain Robert Smith, always known as 'Scraper' in Tynemouth, this would not have been the first time that he had come to London and resignedly found himself being lined up to pose before an eager, if somewhat unmannerly, phalanx of press photographers. On three previous occasions he had come south to be presented with bravery medals, twice for Silver and once for Gold.

His Gold Medal service honoured one of the most famous and significant rescues in the history of the RNLI, an occasion in 1914 which proved, beyond any possible doubt, the superiority of motor-powered lifeboats over their oar- and sail-powered counterparts. The hospital ship *Rohilla*, with 229 medical staff and crew on board was driven on to rocks near Whitby in a gale while on her way to Dunkirk to embark wounded from the Western Front.

Sixty people aboard were drowned almost immediately when the stern section broke away. Thirty-five more were miraculously rescued by one of the Whitby pulling lifeboats before she was too badly damaged to continue. When, after thirty-six hours, the town's second lifeboat and boats from two neighbouring stations were also defeated by the strength of the storm, Tynemouth's motor lifeboat, *Henry Vernon*, was called. Coxswain Smith, together with his station's 'honorary superintendent' Captain H.E. Burton (who was also awarded the Gold Medal for his actions that night), successfully negotiated the 45 miles of coast to Whitby in pitch-darkness, due to wartime blackout, and in gale force winds. There, in fearful conditions, the motor lifeboat was able to get alongside the wreck and take off the remaining survivors.

The unique partnership of a coxswain and an 'honorary superintendent' going to sea together seemed to work well because the two men had already both been awarded Silver Medals the previous year when, in similar conditions, they had taken the same lifeboat, this time north, to Blyth, to rescue the crew of a stranded steamer.

The partnership was actually forged after a period of some difficulty at Tynemouth. In 1905 it had seemed to the RNLI fairly natural to choose Tynemouth as the first station to operate a lifeboat fitted with an experimental motor. After all, the mouth of the Tyne had a proud reputation for innovation. Was it not at South Shields that the first purpose-built lifeboat, the *Original*, had been launched in 1789?

To the Institution's dismay, when the converted pulling lifeboat, the *J. McConnell Hussey*, was delivered to Tynemouth, the volunteer crew would have nothing to do with such a suspect new means of propulsion. The RNLI's initial encouragement had come from H.E. Burton, at that time a lieutenant in the Royal Engineers based in North Shields, a skilled engineer and keen yachtsman who was himself a member of the local RNLI branch.

The lieutenant was determined to prove the worth of the internal combustion engine and defiantly took the lifeboat to sea with a crew of his own sappers. After eight months a sufficient number of local men had been won round by the boat's apparent reliability. They agreed to form a crew on condition that Lieutenant Burton remained 'honorary superintendent' of the lifeboat. 'Scraper' Smith, who had been on the crew of the earlier pulling lifeboat for a good twenty years, was one of the converts and he was eventually made coxswain in 1910.

By the time the photograph on page 30 was taken, Smith had been retired from the lifeboat for four years. It was July 1924 and, as one of the eight men alive to hold the RNLI Gold Medal, he had been invited to London to join in the RNLI's 100th anniversary celebrations. He and six others, including the now promoted Major H.E. Burton and the legendary Henry Blogg of Cromer, were received by King George V at Buckingham Palace and, in the evening of 2 July, attended a banquet at the Hotel Cecil where the RNLI President, Edward, Prince of Wales and Ramsay Macdonald, the Prime Minister, were among the speakers.

Most memorable of all those who rose to address the audience, however, was one Winston Churchill, who would return to political prominence as Chancellor of the Exchequer under Baldwin in October of that year. There is still inspiration to be drawn today from the resounding words he used in the toast he proposed to the RNLI. Here is an extract from his speech:

'Man the lifeboat!' – it is an inspiring call. It may have other applications in daily life. When a friend is in trouble or in sickness, 'Man the lifeboat!' If a class is submerged, ill-treated or exploited, 'Man the lifeboat!' If a small nation is fighting for its life, 'Man the lifeboat!'

All these are applications of the same idea, but the finest of all is the simple actual sphere by the seashore. There is a glorious sphere of heroism and chivalry in human nature. The wreck lies on the reef, great waves are breaking over it, the timbers are going to pieces, the plates are buckling every hour, the crew and the passengers, women and children, are lashed to the rigging, clinging on to any coign of vantage which gives them shelter, or huddled in some structure which has survived the fury of the elements.

There they are, out in the night, in the sea, in the tempest. They have no hope in this world except the lifeboat, but their signals have not been unperceived. The order has gone forth 'Man the lifeboat!' – an order which is never disobeyed.

Great waves may thunder on the shore, winds may drive and beat with their utmost fury, the boat goes out, thrusts its way ahead to the wreck, it is twisted and turned by the convulsions of the sea, it is swamped with water, it is driven back, again and

Launching to a wreck at the mouth of the Tyne in the days before the experimental motor lifeboat was introduced.

again it returns, it pursues and perseveres on its mission of rescue, of salvation to those who are in peril. It drives on with a courage which is stronger than the storm, it drives on with a mercy which does not quail in the presence of death, it drives on as a proof, a symbol, a testimony, that man is created in the image of God, and that valour and virtue have not perished in the British race.

'Scraper' Smith must have been thankful that it was his old shipmate, Major Burton, and not himself who had been asked to follow such oratory by responding on behalf of lifeboat crews. The major coped manfully, however, and ended, 'We have manned your lifeboats for a hundred years. Go on giving us the boats, the best you can – as always – and we will carry on.'

Opposite: The Tynemouth lifeboat, *Henry Vernon*, which motored 45 miles down the coast to Whitby to rescue survivors from the wrecked *Rohilla*.

The 25-knot Severn class lifeboat, *Spirit of Northumberland*, currently serving at Tynemouth.

7 Rescued by the Stromness Lifeboat

The crew of *Carmania II*, 14 February 1929

John William Loftis, skipper of the Grimsby trawler, *Carmania II*, was taking no chances whatsoever. He and his crew of eleven men were on their way home from the fishing grounds off Iceland. They had an excellent catch on board, 500 boxes of cod, and were looking forward to a warm welcome when they eventually got back to their home port.

There was, though, a long and dangerous passage still to negotiate. It was February and the weather was at its worst. Gales had whipped up a very heavy sea and the trawler was making uncomfortable progress towards the ferocious waters that surround the Orkney archipelago. The skipper had been on the bridge without a break for more than twelve hours and he would be staying there until he reached the safety of Stromness Harbour, a staging post on their journey home.

There was not far to go. It was 3.30 a.m. and they had entered Hoy Sound and could see the lights of Graemsay Island. They would soon be turning north towards the shelter of Stromness. Just then every light and every landmark disappeared from sight as a heavy snow shower swept across the Sound. As the skipper and the mate peered through the wheelhouse window for some kind of bearing, they found themselves suddenly thrown across the bridge by an exceptionally heavy sea which shook the trawler with considerable force.

Struggling to regain his balance and the helm, to his alarm the skipper found that the steering gear had jammed. In one brief moment, he had lost all mastery of his fate, his vessel and her crew becoming helpless playthings for the rampaging sea.

They did not have to wait long to discover what mischief it had in store for them. Down below in the engine room, the chief engineer and his mate, oblivious to the desperation of his skipper on the bridge, recalled:

> We both got a shock when we struck. Almost immediately our engines started racing and I knew that our propeller blades were gone. I tried engines

Opposite: Stromness lifeboat manoeuvres close to the *Carmania II*, hard aground on a reef half a mile from the shore.

The Barnett class lifeboat,
J.J.K.S.W., the first 51ft version of
her type, took up duty in Stromness
in 1928.

ahead and astern but they raced either way and we were helpless.

A strong ebb tide had swept the trawler swiftly towards the shore and with a sickening shudder she struck Kirk Rocks, which lie half a mile off the jagged coast of the mainland island of Orkney.

The inhabitants of Innertown, an outlying settlement above the main town of Stromness, would have been fully aware of the wild weather that night. The strong south-westerly wind was carrying snow squalls and the sound of crashing surf straight off the sea and against their windows. Some time just before 4 a.m. a different, piercing and plaintive sound mingled with the roar of wind and waves. It was the sound of a steam-driven siren borne on the wind from the south-west. Concluding swiftly that it could only

mean a ship in peril, three men ran the mile from Innertown to wake up the lifeboat honorary secretary in Stromness.

Immediately the lifeboat crew and the Rocket Lifesaving Brigade were summoned. When they reached the scene, the rocket apparatus team soon realised that they could not help as the trawler was much too far from the shore. The lifeboat coxswain, William Johnston, takes up the story:

It was snowing and very dark. I got my oilskins and made for the lifeboat which was lying at the north pier, never having been housed since our call on Monday night. The rest of the crew came running along and soon we were all aboard. We all know the coast well enough, so made out Hoy Sound about 4.30 a.m.

We could not make out the trawler on the rocks in the darkness but as we got nearer we saw her lights. We motored to the northward in the hope of reaching her for she was lying on a very dangerous skerry. We attempted to reach the trawler but a monster wave made up behind us and broke on board of us, flooding our cockpit aft, so I knew it was impossible to reach her from that direction in the darkness.

Seas were, in fact, breaking 150yds to seaward of the trawler and reefs and shallow water made an approach from between the wreck and the shore equally impossible until the tide rose. The coxswain continues:

I then drew off and dodged about, waiting for daylight and the turn of the tide. We could hear the trawler grinding on the rocks and kent finely that it was all up with her.

As dawn grudgingly broke, the people who had gathered on the shore began to be able to make out the dark shape of the trawler silhouetted against angry white breakers, which swept over the stricken vessel from stem to stern. She rolled and bumped on the rocks with a heavy list and, as the light increased, onlookers could see the men on board her clinging for dear life to the wheelhouse. At one point a huge wave lifted *Carmania II* as though she were a cork, swung her completely round and threw her right on top of the reef.

Aboard *Carmania II* the chief engineer was witnessing the life going out of his vessel:

Our dynamo kept going almost till daylight but finally, as the stokehold became flooded, the fires went out and the head of steam went. Then the dynamo ceased working and all our lights went out. My mate and I sheltered under the whaleback forward but had to leave that for the wheelhouse.

Three hours had passed between the lifeboat's arrival on scene and the moment the coxswain decided he finally had enough light and water beneath him to attempt a rescue. It must have felt more like three days to the men on the trawler.

The coxswain manoeuvred his lifeboat through the massive surf and let go an anchor attached to a wire hawser so that he could veer down stern-first towards the wreck. A line gun was fired towards the trawler but it missed its target. The next two shots succeeded and two lines were secured between the two vessels. This meant a breeches buoy could be rigged and, as the tide rose, the lifeboat was able to veer ever closer to the trawler.

Waves were even greater now as the tide came in. The lifeboat rose high in the air with every sea, then disappeared deep in the trough that followed. Timing was everything for the lifeboat and trawler crews. As a lull came, a man was hauled frantically through the water to the lifeboat's side and pulled, soaking wet and numb with cold, on to the deck.

Five men were safe with seven still to go when a gigantic wave caught the lifeboat nearly broadside on. The wire cable snapped and the lifeboat reeled to leeward. The coxswain's reaction saved his boat and thus the lives of twelve trawlermen and nine lifeboatmen. Still attached to the trawler by the two lines, with perfect seamanship and judgement, he drove his lifeboat full ahead among the reefs and breakers until he was under the lee of the wreck.

Here he saw his opportunity in the shape of a small boat which had been washed from the trawler's deck moments earlier and was now floating under her lee. He shouted to the remaining trawlermen to board her and he would haul them to the lifeboat. In this way, five more men were pulled thankfully aboard. The last two men had just scrambled aboard the small boat when its painter parted and they were swept away.

One of the two men fought to keep the small craft's head to sea with the use of an oar while Coxswain Johnston once again took the considerable risk of steering the lifeboat between

51′ × 13′ 6″ BARNETT TYPE LIFE-BOAT
INSTALLED WITH TWO 60 B.H.P. MOTORS

PROFILE

HALF DECK PLAN

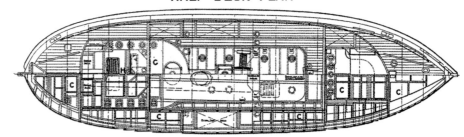

HALF PLAN SHOWING AIR CASES

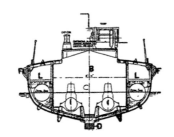

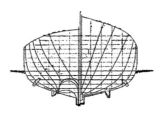

MIDSHIP SECTION

BODY PLAN

A.—Deck.
B.—Engine Room.
C.—Air Cases.
D.—Iron Keel.
E.—End air-compartments.
F.—"Wale" or fender.
G.—Shelter.

H.—Compass and binnacle.
I.—Motor.
J.—Reversing gear.
K.—Propeller.
L.—Petrol tank compartment.
M.—Steering wheel.
O.—Cabin.

A contemporary diagram of the 51ft
Barnett class.

the shore and the casualty. He came alongside the small boat and his crew dragged the survivors on board.

The *Orcadian* newspaper of 21 February 1929 observed somewhat censoriously that among the trawler's crew, landed safely at Stromness that morning, only the mate was a paid-up member of the Shipwrecked Mariners' Society. However, this did not deter the Society's local agent, Mr J.G. Marwick, from providing all twelve men with dry clothes and other necessities, including lodging for the night and money to pay for their journey home. They also received a free examination from the local physician, Dr Cromarty, who prescribed for those who were suffering from exposure.

For one man among the many who raced from Stromness to the cliff-top to witness the rescue, it must have been a traumatic experience. This was the mate of the Grimsby-registered steam ship, *St Malo*, which had been sheltering in Stromness Harbour: the mate's brother was the *Carmania II*'s skipper. He watched the whole episode alongside his skipper who could only declare afterwards that 'Coxswain Johnston deserved a medal. Yes, a medal as big as a frying-pan.'

The coxswain himself would only comment on the performance of his brand new Barnett class lifeboat, *J.J.K.S.W.*, the first 51ft version of the design to be built:

We have a grand boat and we are afraid of nothing above water, if we have plenty of water below us, only keep us off the rocks. Aye, we lost wir anchor and hawser but there's plenty more in London and they'll be on the way north be noo, I'll warrant ye.

His confidence in the RNLI's depot at Poplar was well founded. In reporting the rescue, *The Lifeboat* journal proudly noted that the Stromness honorary secretary had telegraphed the loss of the equipment to the depot on the day of the rescue. The replacement anchor and cable were at once sent by passenger train and arrived in Orkney and were installed aboard the lifeboat within two days.

The *St Malo*'s skipper would not have been disappointed either. For his courage that morning, William Johnston was later awarded a bar to the Bronze Medal he had been awarded seven years earlier when he rescued two men from a raft after their trawler had sunk.

As for the wrecked trawler, the flood tide threw her off the reef and she settled on the bottom of Hellya Sound, between the rocks and the shore, submerged but for the top of her masts, funnel and wheelhouse. A vast, cacophonous flock of seagulls wheeled and whooped around the wreck as quantities of fish were washed into the sea. An even greater prize for the gulls were the cod livers which floated free from barrels washed off the trawler.

8 Boulmer's Sailing Lifeboat

Northumberland, 1930

One of the effects of introducing motor lifeboats into the RNLI fleet was slowly to reduce the frequency of lifeboat stations along the coast. In the nineteenth and early twentieth centuries, few fishing communities, however small, would have been without a pulling and sailing lifeboat. A tour of any part of the British coast today will reveal private dwellings, community halls, seaside cafés, even public lavatories with architectural characteristics betraying their original function as a lifeboat house.

The increased range of the motor lifeboat allowed the RNLI to become more strategic in deciding where to station a boat and it also became clear, by their infrequent use, that some pulling and sailing stations were no longer required. The sparsely populated but treacherous coast of Northumberland, for instance, is nowadays covered by eight all-weather and inshore lifeboat stations; a century ago, there were twice that number.

Whatever the rationale, closing a station has never been an easy option for the RNLI. It inevitably creates local anguish. Along with the church and the village pub, the lifeboat house embodies a community's history and the lifeboat inside is its proud symbol of selfless citizenship and hope for anyone who might need help. At Boulmer in Northumberland, just such a small fishing village lying equidistant on the coast between the Tyne and the Tweed, the local people vowed to retain a lifeboat, independent of the RNLI, when the axe finally fell on them in 1968. The independent station is still in operation today.

Back in 1930 when this photograph was taken, the station was soon to mark its own transition from sail and oar to motor propulsion. The lifeboat, seen returning from an exercise, was the Rubie type, self-righting *Arthur R. Dawes*, built in 1911, which would end her days at Newbiggin, a few miles down the coast, after Boulmer's motor lifeboat arrived in 1931.

She had served the station well, being launched thirty-five times on service and saving the lives of forty-five people. Her coxswain, William Stephenson, earned the RNLI Silver Medal for gallantry aboard her in 1913 when he rescued

Opposite: The letter 'J' is signalled by semaphore to Boulmer pulling and sailing lifeboat, *Arthur R. Dawes*. She was at Boulmer between 1911 and 1931 and launched thirty-five times, saving forty-five lives.

The women launchers at Boulmer.

twenty-five men from the rigging of a French steam trawler, wrecked near Howick Haven in fog. The French government later awarded him a gold medal for the same rescue.

Two families were predominantly involved in manning the Boulmer and neighbouring Alnmouth lifeboats for well over 100 years, the Stephensons who were of Nordic origin and the Stantons whose forebears were Saxon. It was by no means only the men of these two families who got involved. Along with many neighbouring stations, women played a conspicuous part in the dangerous and exhausting work of launching the lifeboat.

One December night in 1925, in a blizzard so fierce that the horses drawing the cart containing stores refused to go on, just about every woman in Boulmer helped to drag the lifeboat over a mile to a suitable launching site. Their route was by a road so narrow that the wheels were continually sinking in the ditches. The women were collectively awarded the RNLI's official thanks on vellum for their pains.

SHIP TO SHORE

Nowadays, only a few people would recognise the letter 'J' being relayed by the man on shore to the lifeboat in the photograph. It may appear somewhat quaint and laborious to the mobile phone generation, but semaphore was a deadly serious means of communication for lifeboat crews in 1930. Visual signals were the only means

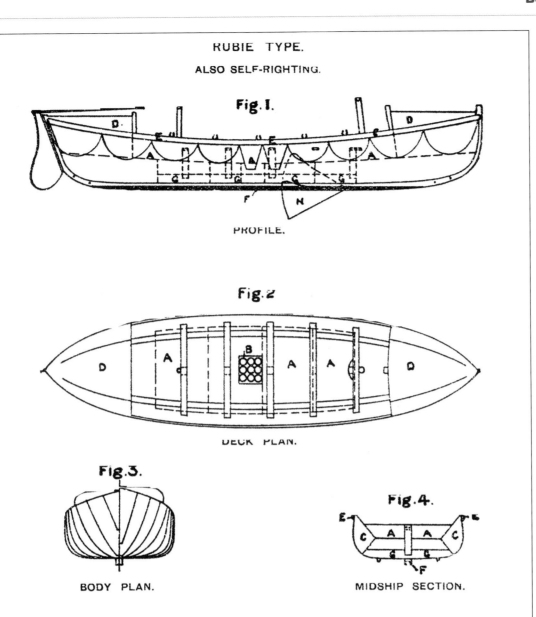

RUBIE TYPE.

ALSO SELF-RIGHTING.

Fig. I.

PROFILE.

Fig. 2

DECK PLAN.

Fig. 3.

BODY PLAN.

Fig. 4.

MIDSHIP SECTION.

A.—Deck.

B.—Relieving valves for the automatic discharge of water off the deck.

C.—Wing air-cases.

D.—End air-boxes, an important factor in self-righting.

E.—" Wale " or " fender."

F.—Iron keel ballast, important in general stability and self-righting.

G.—Water ballast taken in automatically.

H.—Drop-keel.

A contemporary diagram of the Rubie type pulling and sailing lifeboat.

45

A few fishing cobles still operate today at Boulmer.
(*Edward Wake-Walker*)

A landward view of the current Boulmer lifeboat house, operated independently of the RNLI.
(*Edward Wake-Walker*)

of passing messages across the water if you were beyond hailing distance.

The only way to tell a lifeboat far out at sea that she was no longer needed was to fire a recall rocket, but there was never a guarantee the crew had seen it. In one tragic incident in 1928, the lifeboat from Rye Harbour in Sussex launched into a gale to the aid of a vessel whose crew had already got safely ashore. Recall rockets were fired but the lifeboat crew never saw them. Returning from her fruitless search, the pulling and sailing lifeboat capsized and her crew of seventeen were lost.

Morse code flashed by Aldis signal lamps eventually superseded semaphore but in bad visibility and heavy seas, ship-to-shore communication was still often unreliable. (See the 1933 rescue at Cromer of the *Sepoy* on p. 67.) The difficulty of keeping wireless telegraphy and radio telephony equipment dry aboard a lifeboat meant that RNLI vessels had to wait much longer than larger shipping before they could make use of the airwaves for vital links with the shore. The first lifeboat to carry any form of wireless was the Watson Cabin type sent to Rosslare Harbour in Ireland in 1927. She was fitted with a watertight telegraph transmitting and receiving apparatus housed in the comparative shelter of the cabin.

By 1930, five more lifeboats had been fitted, this time with radio telephony equipment. Numbers were still limited because in order to receive transmissions, it was necessary to be within 50 miles of a shore signal station. Also the lifeboat needed a cabin and had to lie afloat, not within a boathouse, so that the mast and aerial could be kept up for regular testing. At the end of 1937, twenty-six boats were equipped with radios and by 1948, with the help of wartime advances in technology, ninety-one motor lifeboats could at least receive radio messages from the shore and most could also transmit them.

9 Named by the Prince of Wales

A Unique Lifeboat for the Dover Strait, 10 July 1930

Even in these twenty-first century days of 25-knot lifeboats, any coxswain will tell you that getting to a casualty quickly is not the be-all and end-all of a successful rescue. He will always sacrifice additional knots for a good sea boat and one that can respond powerfully and nimbly to his command in a tight corner.

Back in 1930, there must have been many a lifeboatman who looked askance at the arrival at Dover of a lifeboat that had been built almost exclusively for speed to the rescue. The traditional view, and one which would continue to influence lifeboat design for the next thirty-five years, was that an effective, safe lifeboat should drive through the water, not skim across it. In the words of the RNLI's journal, *The Lifeboat*, of September 1930,

> The aim of the Institution in the design and construction of motor lifeboats and their engines, which shall be suitable for the work of rescuing life from shipwreck under all conditions, has been, not high speed, but a great reserve of power. It is this reserve of

power, enabling the lifeboat to maintain her speed in the face of the worst conditions of weather, which may make all the difference between success and disaster at that critical moment when a lifeboat is manoeuvring to get alongside or to get away from a wreck.

So what had brought about this brash 17-knot, oversized aberration, capable of nearly twice the speed of any of her noble fellows in the lifeboat fleet and receiving the ultimate accolade of a naming ceremony attended by none other than the heir to the throne, Edward, Prince of Wales, the President of the RNLI? The answer lay in the very special case the Institution's Committee of Management believed existed at Dover.

In spite of the importance of lifeboat cover at one of the busiest ferry-ports in the world and the treachery of the off-lying Goodwin Sands, stationing a lifeboat at Dover had, for some years, been problematic for the Committee. In 1914 the station was forced to close after some sixty years under RNLI jurisdiction. The First World War

Opposite: Edward, Prince of Wales, prepares to release the bottle of champagne which will launch the RNLI's fastest lifeboat into Dover harbour.

The Prince of Wales goes aboard
the visiting French lifeboat, *Maréchal
Foch*, and meets the President of the
French lifeboat society.

was claiming young men from every town and a crew could not be guaranteed at Dover.

In 1919, a steam-driven lifeboat was sent to re-open the station. Only six steam lifeboats were ever built but Dover was considered ideal for one of these 56ft craft with the harbour providing sufficient water at all states of the tide. Also, the vessel's considerable deck space allowed for a large number of survivors should a ferry go down.

By 1922, however, steam lifeboats had gone out of fashion. They had needed four full-time men to maintain them and the internal combustion engine had proved itself to be more versatile and more economical in terms of both manpower and maintenance. The steam lifeboat was withdrawn from Dover and once again the station closed.

The very special case identified by the RNLI for reopening the station in 1930 was the advance of the flying machine. By the late 1920s the aeroplane was becoming a serious alternative means of transport for the well-heeled, if more adventurous traveller. Croydon to Paris in less than two hours was a major selling point for Imperial Airways. But in those early days of aviation, there were still risks in being airborne, not least in the time spent flying over the water. Confidence in the cross-Channel service could not have been enhanced by a report appearing in *The Times* of 22 October 1926 with the headline:

AEROPLANE IN THE CHANNEL.
NARROW ESCAPE OF 12 OCCUPANTS.

The starboard engine of a Handley Page W10 operated by Imperial Airways had suddenly and inexplicably stopped while crossing the Channel the previous afternoon. The plane had been flying low because of bad weather and the pilot soon realised that, with only one engine and losing height, he would not make it to the French coast. He radioed his plight back to Croydon and tugs and boats at Folkestone, Dover and Hythe were

put on alert. He scanned the surface of the sea, but could not find a vessel close to which he could bring his plane down.

When he hit the water, the aeroplane's wings crumpled but the wood of the fuselage and air trapped in parts of the wings and the fuel tanks delayed its immediate sinking. They were a good 18 miles off the English coast and help from that quarter was going to be too slow for the four British and six American passengers, the pilot and the engineer, all huddled on the fast submerging roof of the fuselage.

Very fortunately for them, the skipper of a motor fishing boat, the *Invicta*, had seen the plane heading towards the sea, cut his fishing lines and made all speed to where it had come down. It took them about 25 minutes to cover the 4 miles to the crashed machine, but this was just in time for all the survivors to be taken on board before it sank beneath the waves.

Less than three years later, on the morning of 17 June 1929, another Paris-bound Imperial Airways Handley Page W10, *City of Ottawa*, crashed into the Channel, 3 miles to the east of Dungeness. Although a Belgian trawler, the *Gaby*, came quickly to the rescue and plucked four passengers, the pilot and the mechanic to safety, the seven remaining passengers, who had been sitting in the front of the plane, were drowned. By now, though, the RNLI had responded to what appeared an urgent need to provide an exceptionally fast rescue boat for ditched aircraft.

James Rennie Barnett, the distinguished naval architect who had already designed the widely used 51ft Barnett class lifeboat, was set to work on a very different type of vessel. He was originally asked to come up with a design capable of between 25 and 30 knots but soon convinced his clients that to achieve such performance would mean sacrificing the two essential lifeboat qualities of buoyancy and stability. Thus, in September 1928, the keel of a 64ft vessel, to be

Dover's one-off lifeboat was capable of 17 knots, nearly twice the speed of any other lifeboat built until the 1960s.

capable of 17 to 18 knots, was laid at Thorneycroft's Yard at Hampton-on-Thames.

The oak for the keel came from a 130-year-old tree felled seven years earlier in the Tongues Wood Estate, Hawkhurst, Kent. *The Lifeboat* journal of the day noted that the tree must have been planted a year or two after the first lifeboat, the *Original*, was launched in Tynemouth in 1789. It would have been a flourishing tree when Sir William Hillary founded the RNLI in 1824; most appropriate, as it was his name which the Prince of Wales would be giving to this new boat.

She may have been an unconventional shape but her hull had all the traditional strength of a lifeboat

and more. Mahogany planks were laid double across ribs spaced no more than 9in apart, a quarter of the usual spacing. In all, she weighed 27 tons and was driven by twin Thorneycroft petrol engines, each generating 375hp. Compared with the twin 80hp engines required by the next most powerful lifeboat, the Barnett, it was a massive escalation.

The *Sir William Hillary*'s unusual size meant that she could carry some two hundred survivors at a pinch and could travel a distance of 156 miles at full speed before refuelling. It took seven men to man her, four of whom were permanent crew. She carried every modern aid including line-throwing gun, oil spray for rough water, electric lighting and searchlight and a Marconi two-way radio with a 50-mile range. Her cost, met entirely by the RNLI, was £18,430, nearly two-and-a-half times the sum spent on any previous lifeboat.

It was small wonder, therefore, that every senior official of the RNLI was present at the naming on 7 July 1930, together with top brass from many other organisations including the Deputy Director of Civil Aviation and the Under Secretary of State for Air, both of whom must have been grateful for this new, free service to air travellers.

Intentional or not, the Prince of Wales's arrival at Dover by air lent a certain significance to the arrangements. He landed in a biplane on Swingate Downs having been preceded by other aircraft carrying the government aviation officials. It was a large and illustrious crowd, therefore, that awaited their arrival at the Wellington Dock for the official dedication and naming ceremony to get under way.

The guest list ran like a page of *Debrett's*: Sir Godfrey Baring Bt, Chairman of the RNLI who would officially hand the lifeboat over to the Dover branch; Captain the Right Hon. the Earl Howe, a future chairman who had prepared a vote of thanks for the Prince of Wales; Colonel the Master of Sempill; the Right Hon. Sir Philip Sassoon Bt, MP; Brigadier Sir Hereward Wake Bt and Lady Wake.

The lifeboat's designer, J.R. Barnett, was present, as were Sir John and Lady Thorneycroft. George Shee, Secretary of the RNLI and Captain H.F.J. Rowley, Chief Inspector of Lifeboats kept a watchful eye on the proceedings. Such was the importance of the day that they had invited their French and Dutch counterparts to attend and the President of the French Lifeboat Society was even accompanied by one of his organisation's latest lifeboats, the *Maréchal Foch* which was moored close to the *Sir William Hillary*. Also among the guests of honour sat a Dr C.W. Preston-Hillary,

great-great-grandson of the RNLI's founder. It would have been a proud moment for him and many others present to hear the Prince name the lifeboat and wish:

> God speed to her and all who man her. I feel quite certain she will maintain the best traditions of the lifeboat service and bring new honour to the name she bears.

With those words, he pulled a coloured ribbon and a champagne bottle fell with precision and smashed across the lifeboat's bow. Then he stepped forward to cut a second ribbon and the *Sir William Hillary* slid gracefully away from him, stern first into the harbour.

There was, in fact, never to be another lifeboat of this design built. The *Sir William Hillary* spent barely ten years at Dover, during which time she answered forty-three calls and saved twenty-nine lives. This included one service, just after the outbreak of war in 1939, to a trawler, *Blackburn Rovers*, which had fouled her propeller and was dragging her anchor through a minefield while carrying out anti-submarine work for the Admiralty. The Dover lifeboat reached the trawler in heavy seas and a gale and, with great difficulty and at enormous risk, took off the sixteen-man crew, together with their ship's papers and secret gear. Coxswain Colin Bryant was awarded the Silver Medal for bravery and three of his crew the Bronze for this rescue.

In 1940 it was decided that the military should take responsibility for all air–sea rescue operations and so this specialised lifeboat was sold to the Admiralty, who used her around the coast of Britain for that purpose. Ironically, she was not once called to assist a downed aircraft during all the time she was the Dover lifeboat.

The next time the RNLI was to operate a lifeboat capable of more than 9 knots was in 1967 when the 15-knot Waveney class was introduced, based on a US coastguard surf-boat design.

10 On the Rocks

The Steamer *Benmohr* at Prawle Point, Devon, 25 February 1931

The pessimists aboard the SS *Benmohr*, a twin-screw steamer of the renowned Ben Line of Leith, would not have been surprised by the dour welcome they received as their 6,000-ton vessel headed into the western approaches to the English Channel. It was February, after all. They were bound for Dunkirk on the last leg of a voyage which had started at Dunedin in New Zealand, more than seven weeks earlier.

The vessel was in ballast and responded with a lively motion to the heavy following seas, which goaded her eastwards up the Channel. Added impetus, however, was the last thing the captain wanted at this moment. A blanket of dense fog, spread across the entire south-west of the British Isles over the past few days, was making navigation a grim game of Russian roulette for all shipping in the area. Already, a schooner, the *Julia*, had been driven blindly on to the Arklow Bank with the loss of her skipper and crew of five.

The *Benmohr*'s captain had slowed his engines to a crawl and was feeling his way up the Channel. With visibility at only 100yds, he had precious little to guide him. It was late afternoon and what dim light was left would only have shown him the white-capped seas around his vessel. His compass would have confirmed his north-easterly course, but he had no bearings so could not be sure of his position.

All ships of those days bound up-Channel would make for Prawle Point Signal Station, the most southerly point on the Devon coast, to give their recognition signals. In the fog, all that the *Benmohr* could rely upon was sound. There were many on shore that afternoon who heard the steamer's siren as she crept up the Channel, her crew straining to hear an answering call from Prawle Point. But the strong wind from the west carried the sound away from the ship until she was level with the station.

At around 5 p.m. that same wind carried the sound of the *Benmohr*'s siren, this time blasting an urgent distress signal, towards the coastguard lookout at Prawle Point. She was aground. She had struck below the steep, jagged cliffs at Islands Lake, just to the west of the Point. Had she made it a few hundred yards to the south, she would have cleared Prawle Point with open water ahead of her.

As it was, when the first rescuers arrived on the cliff-top, they were astonished to make out through the rain and fog, a ship lying practically on top of the wreck of the *Ida*, which had run ashore there only a few months earlier. To begin with, her stern remained in deep water but soon the strong north-westerly wind drove her broadside to the shore and she became firmly fixed amidships, her stern nearest to the land.

Opposite: The steamship, *Benmohr*, hard aground at the foot of the cliffs at Prawle Point.

Salcombe's coxswain, Eddie Distin.

Opposite, top: The Salcombe lifeboat, *William and Emma*, which capsized in 1916 and from which Eddie Distin was one of the only two survivors.

Opposite, bottom: Wreckage from a 1990s casualty deposited high up the rocks at the exact place where the *Benmohr* struck in 1931. The wreckage is from the Chinese-owned cargo ship *Demetrios*, which broke loose from a Russian tug in a Force 10 gale on 18 December 1992, while being towed to Turkey to be scrapped. (*Edward Wake-Walker*)

Before long, a sizeable gathering of local cottagers had assembled on the cliff, many of whom had carried with them clothing, brandy and other necessities for anyone brought ashore. Meanwhile, a maroon had been fired to summon both the lifeboat at Salcombe and the rocket apparatus crew at Prawle village.

The rocket crew piled their apparatus on to a cart and set off across rain-sodden fields to cover the mile and a quarter distance to the stricken ship. It was very dark when they arrived at the scene but in spite of this and the very limited visibility, the men rigged up their apparatus and pointed the rocket at the *Benmohr*. In a shower of golden sparks, the rocket flew seaward, carrying its line directly across the steamer, some 200yds away. Her crew then heaved a heavier line aboard, the breeches buoy was run out and all was set for men to be brought ashore.

Down at Salcombe lifeboat station hearts were beating fast; crew members dashed through the streets, pulling on extra clothing as they went, other

villagers looking on anxiously. This was the very first shout since the station had reopened, two months previously. For the first time a motor lifeboat, the 40ft, self-righting *Alfred and Clara Heath* would be put to the test at Salcombe. In command was Edwin Distin, a man who, until this moment, had only known rescue under sail and oar.

Distin's credentials for the task ahead, however, were second to none. Before the station's five-year closure, he had been coxswain of the pulling lifeboat. He had taken up the appointment immediately following the tragic loss of thirteen men from the Salcombe lifeboat after she capsized in October 1916, on a mission to the grounded schooner, *Western Lass*. Only two men had survived the disaster; Edwin Distin was one of them.

Now he found himself heading out across the bar, making for the very spot where, in similar bleak conditions, he had fought for his life in the water fifteen years earlier. His greatest problem was the fog and it took all his local knowledge to edge along the coast until they found the *Benmohr*. By this time, it was about 6.30 p.m. and in the beam of floodlights from the steamer the lifeboat crew could make out the line running between ship and shore. There seemed to be little activity, however, and as the coxswain drew close to the casualty's side to investigate, an unseen swell picked up the *Benmohr* and heeled her over so far that she struck the lifeboat. The coxswain pulled away and soon ascertained by semaphore the reason for the inactivity: the captain had ordered all his crew to stay on board. He was determined to save his ship and was now awaiting the arrival of salvage tugs from Falmouth.

The lifeboat stood off and also waited for the tugs to come. There was a hope that the ship could be refloated on the high tide at midnight. Unfortunately, the tugs did not arrive in time for that and so she was still there the next morning, her bow now pointing out to sea and her stern closer still to the cliffs. The lifeboat had returned to her station in the early hours, once the tugs had reached the scene, but the rocket crew kept up their cliff-top vigil throughout the night.

During the next day the weather worsened and waves crashed against the rocks in 25ft of spray. Finally, in the afternoon, the captain relented and forty-two men were hauled by breeches buoy

from the steamer. It was a textbook operation, which took Mr Catchpole, the chief officer of the Prawle Point coastguard, only 50 minutes to accomplish. His rescue party had been waiting for this moment, exposed to the winter elements for the last twenty-four hours.

The captain, his chief steward, the cook, boatswain and radio operator remained on board. Eventually the weather relented and a few days later the *Benmohr* was floated off the rocks on a high tide. She continued to ply her trade for another eleven years until, on 5 March 1942, UK-bound from Bombay and 235 miles south-east of Freetown on the West African coast, she was torpedoed, the very first victim of a newly commissioned German U-boat, *U-505*. Fifty-six people made it to the boats and by sheer chance were spotted the next day by a Sunderland flying boat. With some difficulty, the plane landed, picked up the survivors and flew them on to Freetown and safety.

11 Wrecked Beneath the Cliffs

The schooner *Sarah Evans* near Portreath, 30 October 1932

Today, to appreciate the dramatic, bleak beauty of the stretch of coastline between Portreath and Porthtowan on the north Cornish coast you must be prepared to walk. No road or track leads straight to it and the only way to experience the giddy feeling of looking 350ft down on to the sea from sheer cliff-tops is to take the coastal path as it winds steeply up out of one of the villages at either end.

In 1932, there was not even an official coastal path. However, that did not deter some two thousand people from the neighbourhood leaving their homes on an October Sunday afternoon during one of the worst gales anyone could remember, and scrambling across the rugged, precipitous terrain to witness the fate of a stranded schooner.

She was the *Sarah Evans*, an Appledore-based motor schooner that had sailed from Newport, South Wales, on the previous Friday evening with a cargo of coal, bound for Par, near St Austell on the south coast of Cornwall. By the Saturday evening, her skipper, William Hopkins, found himself heading into the teeth of a ferocious south-westerly gale. He informed his mate and the other crew member that if they could, they would put into Padstow. But when they got there, the weather made it too dangerous to come inshore and attempt entering the Camel estuary, so there was no option but to plough on. The wind began to turn more northerly and this encouraged the skipper to hope that his auxiliary engine would be enough to keep him off the lee shore, and that he could make it round Land's End into safer waters.

All Saturday night the *Sarah Evans* battled on through towering seas, making precious little headway, but at least keeping a safe distance from the shore. By daybreak on Sunday, as the vessel teetered on the crest of a wave, the three men aboard could glimpse the grey outline of St Agnes Head off their port bow. Then came the inevitable nose-dive as the schooner once again buried her bowsprit deep into the base of the next oncoming mountain of water.

Throughout the previous night, one modest sound above all the chaos of wind and sea had kept the men sane. It was the gentle throbbing of the auxiliary motor, persevering heroically against the elements and drumming out a message of reassurance to the crew.

Opposite: The *Sarah Evans* moments before she began to break up. It is just possible to make out the cliff rescuers and their ladder and ropes on the extreme right of the photograph.

At eight o'clock in the morning, abruptly it stopped. Every possible idea was tried, every prayer offered up and every oath uttered, but the engine had fired its last. There was no need to look; the men knew that with each minute the jagged granite coastline to the south of them was looming larger, like the opening jaw of a hungry beast of prey.

Desperately, as winds reached 80mph, the schooner's crew fought to put their vessel under sail but in the skipper's own words:

> . . . From that time it seemed pretty hopeless. We were battling for hours, hoping for the best. Two of our sails were blown away and then we tried to put up the balloon sail but that was no sooner up than it was carried away. We let out the starboard anchor, which was scarcely down before it went, and the other anchor dragged and we drifted. Then we could do nothing to keep the boat out of the bay and at about two o'clock we put up the red flag.

In almost immediate response to this signal of distress, there was an explosion at the top of the cliff which now towered above the schooner and a missile with line attached hurtled towards her. It was a highly accurate shot and the crew were able to grab the line from the sea with a boathook. Maybe, after all, they still had a chance.

Ashore, the rescue parties were doing everything they could to give them that chance. Portreath coastguards had realised for some hours that they had a virtually inevitable shipwreck on their hands. Two lifeboats had been standing by and immediately they were told the signal requesting assistance had been flown, they launched.

One was the *Princess Mary*, Padstow's 61ft Barnett class motor lifeboat and the other, the veteran twelve-oared pulling and sailing *James Stevens No. 10*, stationed at St Ives and under the command of Coxswain Tommy Cocking. Both lifeboat crews had a gruelling passage ahead of them, especially the men of St Ives who had no shelter and only their own muscle power and sailing skills to rely upon.

In the event, and in spite of heroic feats of endurance, neither crew was even to get a sight of the wreck. Padstow lifeboat had battled as far as St Agnes Head before she received a message to say she was no longer needed. The men of St Ives

actually reached the reported position of the wreck but, such were the conditions, they could see no sign of the schooner and continued 2 miles beyond St Agnes before receiving a recall signal and fighting their way back to St Ives. Both crews had spent five hours at sea in appalling weather with nothing to show for their efforts.

They did not yet know what had transpired at the cliff-face. At the moment that the line was established between the *Sarah Evans* and the rocket crew, the vessel was barely a cable's length (200yds) from the shore. But she was still drifting rapidly towards the tiny Wheal Sally Cove. Before there was time to rig the breeches buoy, the line snagged on the cliff as the schooner was swept round a small headland and into the cove. It was now useless.

A horrifying sight met the crowds of people on the cliff-top as they craned forward over the precipice, struggling to keep a foothold as the wind strove to hurl them off balance. Huge breakers thundered down upon the sailing ship, swamping her deck before rolling disdainfully on to the ragged shore where they exploded in a plume of white spray. Within minutes now the *Sarah Evans* would be crashing against those very rocks herself.

Then they saw three tiny figures emerge on to the deck, swing their legs over the gunwales and throw themselves into the water. They were immediately picked up in the surf and swept uncontrollably towards the cliff-face. The men had seen a little strip of sand and hoped to be deposited there but each time they came close, a reflected wave would carry them back towards their abandoned vessel.

Miraculously, all three men made it to the beach but one of them, the skipper, was so exhausted that he lay flat on the sand, unable to move another inch. His two shipmates used all their remaining willpower and strength to haul their captain to his feet; they knew that the tide was coming in and they needed to get as high as they could. So sheer were the cliffs all around them that they could get no higher than 10ft above the beach – and that would afford no protection when the tide came in.

Their lives depended on the people at the top of the cliff who knew that they had little time in

which to act. It was a vertical drop down to where the three survivors huddled and there were no footholds to be gained on the soft, crumbling face of the cliff. Eight men stepped forward to volunteer to be lowered down the cliff-face by rope. They were: Police Constable Mutton, Chief Coastguard Baker, Captain Wilson, W.A. Buston, all of St Agnes; R. Nicholls, J. Williams, B. Williams of Portreath and H. Tonkin of Porthtowan.

The men let themselves be lowered down the face of rock inch by inch, occasionally dislodging stones which hurtled down, hitting one of their fellows below. With great difficulty, ropes were manoeuvred into the hands of the shipwrecked crew who put them around their waists. They then half scrambled and were half hauled up to a

rope ladder which had been lowered from the top. The whole operation took about an hour but at the end of it, everyone was back at the top, uninjured except for some cuts and bruises.

The three survivors were in a state of utter exhaustion and had not eaten for thirty hours. They were carried by stretcher to awaiting ambulances which took them to the Basset Arms Hotel in Portreath to recover from their ordeal.

Minutes after the crew of the *Sarah Evans* had crawled ashore, their vessel was aground. She was rocked violently in the wind and seas broke completely over her as she rapidly began to break up. By the time the survivors were carried from the cliff-top, she had gone completely to pieces and disappeared, leaving only a black smudge of coal dust on the surface of the water.

St Ives pulling lifeboat, *James Stevens No. 10*. Her crew reached the position of the wreck but could see nothing in the conditions.

12 Wrecked on South Beach

The herring drifter *Olive*, Great Yarmouth, 20 October 1933

There has probably been no greater influence on the shaping of coastal communities in northern and eastern Britain over recent centuries than the humble herring. This once plentiful cousin of the mackerel, pilchard and sprat that roamed the North and Irish Seas in huge shoals, provided a cheap and nutritious source of food and was consumed freshly grilled, smoked, tinned, salted, pickled or even raw in households throughout the United Kingdom and Europe.

By the end of the nineteenth century, many east-coast harbours had been enlarged to accommodate the ever-growing fleet of herring drifters. These boats would chase the migrating shoals of 'silver darlings' from Shetland and Orkney in the spring to East Anglian waters in the autumn. A large proportion of the drifters were Scottish based, but their presence helped to build the economy of every port where their catch was landed, and none more so than Lowestoft and Great Yarmouth.

As well as giving trade to all the ancillary businesses such as victuallers, chandlers and boat repairers, these vessels brought work for thousands in gutting, processing and curing the herring.

When the Scottish boats arrived in the autumn, they would be followed by train and lorry loads of Scots fishergirls whose labour was required to cope with the millions of additional fish brought ashore.

The arrival of steam-powered drifters at the turn of the twentieth century brought the herring industry to a peak of activity around 1910. In that year Great Yarmouth boasted 1,000 of its own registered drifters but also needed to service a further 2,000 Scottish boats. In the autumn, the harbour would become so crowded that it was possible to walk across the boats from one side of it to the other.

Steam drifters became popular very rapidly. Although, at £4,000, they were about three times as costly as their sail-driven predecessors, at 90ft they were longer, so could carry more fish; they were less at the mercy of wind and tide; they could travel much more rapidly from fishing ground to port and back and they were fitted with steam-driven capstans to haul in the nets.

Theirs was a very familiar shape with a mizzen sail, used to steady the boat when its nets were out, and a thin, tall funnel, like a smoking cigarette, designed to carry the steam and fumes high above and away from the crew working

Opposite: The herring drifter, *Olive*, is demolished by the sea after she ran on to the South Beach at Great Yarmouth.

Coxswain William Fleming, holder of the Bronze, Silver and Gold RNLI bravery medals. The Gold was awarded after a rescue lasting two nights and a day in a fierce north-easterly gale aboard the Gorleston pulling lifeboat in 1922. The whole twenty-four-man crew of the steamer *Hopelyn* was safely brought ashore.

Great Yarmouth and Gorleston motor lifeboat, *John and Mary Meiklam of Gladswood*. She was of the broad-beamed 'Norfolk and Suffolk' design.

curtain just below the surface of the sea. The vessel would then drift with the tide with its net stretching up to a mile out astern, while the herring came to the surface at dusk to feed on plankton. Their fate was to swim into the net and be caught by the gills.

By 1933 the heyday of the herring industry had passed. Over-fishing had begun to take its toll but, more importantly, Germany and Russia, once both prolific consumers of cured herring, were no longer able to afford food from abroad as Germany's postwar and Russia's post-Revolution economies struggled. Catches were therefore less and prices were lower.

As he hauled in his net with its meagre harvest of seven crans* of herring and set a course for Great Yarmouth, Alexander Smith, the ageing skipper and owner of the Banff-registered steam drifter, *Olive*, calculated that he would barely be covering the cost of his night's work. His thirty-year-old vessel with its coal-fired steam engine and ten-man crew was finding it hard to compete with the modern motor-driven boats which needed fewer men and cost much less in fuel.

To add to his woes, it was a filthy night. A gale had sprung up from the south-east and as his 31-ton vessel began to corkscrew violently in the heavy seas, the skipper realised with increasing

on deck. Many people referred to them as 'Woodbines' because of their funnel.

Their actual method of fishing was no different from that used by the earlier sailing boats. Long nets would be paid out so that they hung down like a

* A cran is equivalent to four baskets; a basket holds approximately 250 herring.

View of the harbour entrance at
Great Yarmouth.

apprehension that he would have a job on his hands when he reached the harbour entrance at Yarmouth.

A time will come when even the most experienced and skilful seamen run out of luck. Wind and seas were running diagonally across the narrow entrance as the *Olive* lined herself up with the light on the southern arm of the harbour. The elements were conspiring to sweep the drifter across the entrance and Alexander Smith knew that he would have to judge his moment precisely to make his dash across the bar. He scoured the sea in the darkness, looking for a gap in the waves, then he made his move.

But he was deceived; just as he drew level with the two piers, a huge sea loomed up on the drifter's port stern quarter, picked her up and flung her stern against the north pier with agonising force. It was soon obvious to all on board that their boat was now badly holed and that she was entirely at the mercy of the sea. The impact with the harbour wall had turned the vessel completely round so that she now faced north and the seas that crashed down upon her were driving her out of the harbour and into the breakers on the beach to the north.

The town soon knew that someone was in trouble that night when they heard urgent blasts from the *Olive*'s siren. Within minutes the Great Yarmouth and Gorleston lifeboat had left her station and was powering down the river towards the open sea. Coxswain William Fleming, holder of the RNLI's Gold, Silver and Bronze bravery

medals, turned the lifeboat hard to port to round the north pier and almost immediately his crew could make out the drifter, aground on a sandbank with breakers washing over her.

Quickly, Fleming put an anchor down to seaward of the casualty and veered down towards the shallow water where she lay. But even before he could get close, the *Olive* was dislodged from the bank by the waves and driven, semi-submerged, on to the beach amid the breakers where she lay in a few feet of water. The lifeboat would have run aground before she got anywhere near her.

Very fortunately for the *Olive*'s skipper and crew, she was now so close to the beach that the coastguard shore party were able to get a line aboard her and all ten men were hauled through the surf to safety via breeches buoy. Clutching some of their clothes and personal possessions, they were bundled into waiting motor cars and taken to the Sailors' Home for a hot bath and a few hours' sleep.

Later that morning, the crew joined the many spectators and the local journalist on the beach to inspect what was left of their vessel. It was a sorry sight as seas broke over her waterlogged hull, with parts of her bulwarks already torn away by their ferocity. Seagulls circled her decks, anticipating the feast that would be served up to them as she slowly yielded her haul of fish to the breakers. As he gazed at his ruined livelihood, Alexander Smith would only comment: 'It might have been worse.'

13 Aground off Cromer

The sailing barge *Sepoy*, 13 December 1933

For two British vessels, both plying their trade on the east coast of England and both caught in a vicious easterly gale which sprang up without warning during the night, 13 December 1933 proved to be a tragically unlucky day. People on the beach at Aldeburgh in Suffolk watched through their binoculars as the steamship *Culmore* of Londonderry heeled over and sank with all nine hands still on board. By the time the lifeboat had launched, no trace of the ship was to be found.

All thirteen men aboard the *Broomfleet* of Goole were lost when she vanished after leaving the Humber on the same day, bound for Ipswich. The bodies of her crew were later washed ashore on the Norfolk coast. Five Norfolk lifeboats gave gallant service to other casualties of the gale, but none more so than the crew of the Cromer motor lifeboat, *H.F. Bailey*, under the command of Coxswain Henry Blogg.

Blogg and his crew were first called from their beds at four in the morning. When they arrived at the boathouse, perched on the end of Cromer pier, they learned that a vessel was burning flares off Happisburgh, about 11 miles to the south-east

along the coast. Huge seas surged towards the beach under the planking of the pier as they donned oilskins and lifejackets. They had already felt the iciness of the spray-filled wind against their faces; soon they would be afloat in the darkness and entirely at the mercy of the gale.

After two hours battling into the sea and wind, the lifeboat came upon the spritsail barge, *Glenway*, driven ashore and lying in water far too shallow for the lifeboat to get alongside. The tide was ebbing and Coxswain Blogg stood off in deeper water and was eventually rewarded by the sight of the skipper, mate and ship's boy walking ashore, carrying the ship's cat, as the tide left the barge high and dry.

Their job may have been done, but the lifeboat crew knew that they still had much to endure. The weather would not allow the lifeboat to be rehoused at the top of her slipway in Cromer; instead, she would have to continue on along the coast to the nearest harbour which was Gorleston, another 17 miles into the teeth of the gale. Heavy seas continually swept over the lifeboat as she headed south-east, drenching each man on board and chilling him to the bone.

Opposite: A rocket is fired from Cromer beach towards the stricken Thames barge, *Sepoy*. The line attached to the rocket is just visible to the right of the smoke. Meanwhile, Cromer's pulling lifeboat, the *Alexandra*, is brought to the water's edge.

Launchers tow Cromer's pulling lifeboat, *Alexandra*, across the beach.

As he passed the coastguard station at Sea Palling, the coxswain flashed a message to check he was not needed for any further call back at Cromer, but the conditions were so bad that neither lifeboat nor coastguard could read the other's signal. The lifeboat ploughed on, therefore, towards Gorleston.

Henry Blogg had probably been thinking about another barge that had been kept under close observation by the Cromer coastguard throughout the previous night. She had been at anchor about a mile and a half east of Cromer pier and was in considerable danger as the wind increased. The barge was the *Sepoy* of Dover and Blogg was right to have been concerned on her behalf. Her captain,

Joseph Hempstead of Grays in Essex, was later to broadcast an account of his experience on the BBC:

This is 'Old Joe' speaking, skipper of the *Sepoy*. Our trouble started by us blowing a joint off the Humber on Monday afternoon, which put the engine out of action. There was a thick haze about, and a nor'-west wind, not no gale then.

There was only two of us aboard – myself and mate, Jack Stevenson, a young chap of twenty – and we were carrying 144 tons of tiles. We sailed along and anchored, on Tuesday afternoon, off Cromer, when the tide stopped coming with us; four hours later, at about nine o'clock, the wind sprang up from the eastward and increased quickly to a gale. We gave her 80 fathoms chain on the bow anchor, and paid away on both chains, as we were driving a bit.

The gale gradually got worse and I saw it was time to do something, so I flared several times. But there was no response to our appeal.* By this time the wind had driven us well into the shore – it was bitterly cold, and the sea was very rough. When daylight came we hoisted a distress signal. The sea was increasing and we were now about a quarter of a mile off the shore, and getting low in the water.

At about eleven o'clock she was almost sunk and struck the ground. Up to about daylight we had been up and down on deck, seeing that things were secure, but after this time the seas began to come right over and we had to take to the rigging and stay there. We could see on the shore that they were now trying to launch the lifeboat.

The lifeboat which the two bargemen saw was the town's veteran pulling and sailing boat, the *Alexandra*, built in 1902 and, in keeping with many stations where a motor lifeboat had been introduced, kept as a back-up in case of engine problems in the No. 1 boat.

Had Henry Blogg been able to read the signal flashed by the coastguard at Sea Palling, he would have known that the station was urgently recalling him to help the *Sepoy*. As it was, he was steaming on towards Gorleston and so the pulling lifeboat, along with the lifesaving apparatus team, appeared to be the only hope for the two men clinging to the rigging of the barge.

The *Alexandra* was wheeled down to the water's edge on her carriage with the help of a hundred willing volunteers. Robert Davies, who had been forced to retire as mechanic from the lifeboat crew because of bad eyesight, was to take the helm in the absence of Henry Blogg and his crew. The crew was made up of local fishermen and members of the shore lifesaving team.

On the first attempt to launch the lifeboat, she was immediately washed back broadside on to the beach by the colossal surf. Launchers hauled her back on to her carriage and she was once more pushed out into the sea and tipped into the waves. This time her crew at the oars kept her afloat in the surf for 20 minutes, but they could make no headway and she was eventually driven back on to

the shingle. Again she was manhandled back on the carriage and this time dragged along the beach for half a mile to a position further to windward of the wreck. Meanwhile, on their fourth attempt, the lifesaving company had just succeeded in landing a rocket-line across the *Sepoy*. The lifeboat also made it through the surf this time and her crew fought manfully to get close to the barge.

By now it was two o'clock in the afternoon and Joe Hempstead and his mate had been three hours in the rigging. The skipper relates what happened after the line landed across his vessel:

My mate pluckily got down from the rigging and crawled along the foredeck to the stern and got hold of the line. This sounds easier in the telling than the doing. The barge was rolling very badly and I shouted to him: 'Look out Jack. Hold tight.'

He laid flat and held on while the sea went right over him. Then he scrambled up and got aloft and I nipped down the rigging too and got the line from him. We went back up the rigging with it and hauled aboard.

By this time the lifeboat was afloat and drifting down past us. Unfortunately, it fouled the rocket-line which we'd just secured and broke it, cutting off all connection. The main hatch-cloth had just washed out of the battens and, of course, the barge was soon full of water. She now began to bump, heaving up and down on the ground, which made it much more difficult for us to hang on to the rigging. The lifeboat had been washed up again on to the beach and our chances didn't look too rosy.

My mate was getting exhausted by the strain and cold and when he said: 'Here's a lifeboat coming – it's all right', I said: 'Stick it, Jack', because I couldn't see anything. But he was higher up the rigging than I and could see better. He was right. This was the motor lifeboat of Cromer coming to our assistance.

A telephone call to Gorleston coastguard was what led, at last, to the return of Henry Blogg and his crew to Cromer. The coastguard relayed the message to Great Yarmouth and Gorleston lifeboat station whose crew straightaway launched their motor lifeboat, *John and Mary Meiklam of Gladswood*, to intercept Henry Blogg before he arrived. If his crew were too exhausted to return, the Great Yarmouth and Gorleston boat would make for Cromer herself.

* Coastguards and townspeople saw nothing but the anchor light burning throughout the night, in spite of their concern for the vessel.

When the two lifeboats met near the Cockle lightship, 8 miles from Gorleston, there was no question in Henry Blogg's mind but that he should turn back immediately to cover the 20 miles of gale-whipped seas that lay between him and the *Sepoy*. The time was 11.30 a.m., the gale was at its height and he and his men had been out in it for seven hours already.

Two and a half hours later, Blogg was in sight of the wreck and sizing up a way of getting alongside. Her decks were completely submerged, with huge waves sweeping over her. The position of her anchor cables made it impossible for the lifeboat to anchor to windward and drop down on her. The only possible approach was round the barge's stern and running in alongside to the leeward, through the heavy surf between the barge and the shore. There was a great risk of capsize as it meant coming broadside on to the seas. Several times the coxswain attempted the manoeuvre, but he was continually swept past the wreck. Finally, the lifeboat got close enough for a grapnel to be thrown into the rigging, but just then a big sea flung her against the wreck, her side was holed and the grapnel line parted.

Time was now running out. The two men could not possibly hang on much longer in the rigging. Throwing caution to the wind, Coxswain Blogg drove his lifeboat straight on to the deck of the barge, stoving in her bulwarks close to the rigging where the men were perched. The *Sepoy* skipper recalls this dramatic moment:

> I said: 'Jump, Jack.' He was just about done up, and he seemed inclined to hold on to the backstay but just as the lifeboat came up on the swell, he reached up and they grabbed his arm and pulled him aboard.

The lifeboat was then swept off the deck of the barge but the coxswain brought her up and drove her a second time over the wreck. Hempstead grabbed a stanchion with his left hand and a lifeboat crewman took his right arm and he, too, was pulled unceremoniously aboard.

This time there was no question of the lifeboat going to Gorleston. The survivors needed urgent medical attention. The crew had been at sea for eleven hours. Blogg steered straight for the shore and beached the lifeboat. People rushed into the surf to steady her while the rescued men were

brought ashore. The mate was carried on a stretcher but the skipper was still able to walk. As he hobbled across the beach, the sound of Cromer church bells rang out in celebration of the rescue.

The two bargemen soon recovered from their ordeal and in his BBC broadcast, Joe Hempstead finished by thanking

> . . . all the kind friends who've sent me letters of sympathy, Commander Harrison of the Shipwrecked Mariners Society, which does so much good all round our coast and, last but not least, Coxswain Blogg of the Cromer lifeboat and his gallant crew. And what I'm doing here, I don't know. My pals'll think me a fool; but I'm not the first who's been shipwrecked, nor the last.

Henry Blogg, already the holder of two RNLI Gold Medals and one Silver for bravery, was awarded his second Silver Medal for this rescue. His crew, together with Robert Davies who had command of the pulling and sailing lifeboat, all received the official thanks of the RNLI inscribed on vellum. In an interview with the press after the rescue, Blogg was characteristically dismissive about the seamanship he had displayed in carrying out the rescue, but he did allow that the 'journey up and down' to Gorleston had been one of the worst in his twenty-four years as coxswain.

This page and opposite: The *Sepoy* is swamped; her crew are in the rigging. Cromer motor lifeboat *H.F. Bailey* makes her daring approach and is driven on to the deck of the barge.

14 Trouble in Filey Bay

The steamer *Garthclyde*, 1 February 1934

There is precious little shelter to be found on the Yorkshire coast north of Flamborough Head when you are heading into a strengthening northerly wind. The 250-ton, oil-driven steamer *Garthclyde*, which had begun her voyage from Norwich along the peaceful waters of the River Yare, found herself, on the late afternoon of Wednesday 31 January 1934, struggling in heavy seas and making little headway towards her destination of Blyth in Northumberland.

Looking landward towards the wide sweep of Filey Bay, the steamer's skipper, A.V. Grantham, reckoned that if he were to anchor and wait for more favourable conditions, it would have to be off the town of Filey to the north of the bay, in the lee offered by the narrow promontory of Filey Brigg. This he decided to do, but soon realised that the anchorage was not as safe as he had hoped. The ship was rolling heavily and he let go a second anchor. Out of the darkness, he thought he could see the occasional flash of signals coming from the coastguard station but he could not decipher their message. He was also pretty certain they could not make out his reply. There was nothing to do but wait for the morning and hope that the anchors would hold sufficiently and that the gale that was now blowing would subside. Had he known the weather was going to get so bad, he would have made for Bridlington, further south, under the far more substantial shelter of Flamborough Head.

By daybreak matters were, if anything, worse. The wind had shifted to the north-east, exposing his ship to the full fury of the North Sea. There were still 3 fathoms of water under Skipper Grantham's keel, but with no lee offered by the land, he could no longer trust his anchors to keep his ship and his crew of four safe. The repeated semaphore message conveyed by a man silhouetted on the steamer's deck and signal flags hoisted on the mast removed all doubt in the mind of the coastguard lookout as to what was required. The *Garthclyde*'s men wished to be taken off.

The tractor was hitched to the lifeboat carriage and soon Filey's pulling and sailing lifeboat, *Hollon the Third*, had descended the ramp from the seafront promenade and was crossing the broad, sandy beach towards the icy water's edge. In close attendance strode her coxswain, Dicky

Opposite: The crew of the *Garthclyde* come ashore without even getting their feet wet.

The narrow promontory of Filey Brigg.

Jenkinson and his crew, strapping on their kapok lifejackets and peering out across the breakers at the dark shape of the *Garthclyde* as she strained on her anchor cables, only a few hundred yards away.

It still took the men at the oars some 20 minutes to cover the distance, pulling hard to keep the lifeboat's head to sea through the surf and heavy seas. Once alongside the steamer, it did not take long to embark her captain and four crewmen and, within an hour of the lifeboat launching to their assistance, they were ashore, as the picture shows, without even getting their feet wet.

To Skipper Grantham's considerable relief, the weather improved later that day, his vessel remained afloat, and he and his crew were put back aboard to continue their passage up the coast.

Filey lifeboat, *Hollon the Third*, being hauled by an early RNLI tractor from her shed in 1932.

15 The First Motor Lifeboat Rescue

Flamborough Head, 4 January 1935

Most of the four hundred fishermen who, in the late nineteenth century, lived on the wild, chalk-cliff peninsula of Flamborough Head, just north of Bridlington in Yorkshire, used to keep two fishing cobles, one at North Landing and one on the other side of the Head at South Landing. It meant that they could nearly always get a boat away, whatever the wind direction.

In 1871, soon after the Great Gale in Bridlington Bay which had wrecked thirty ships sheltering there with the loss of seventy lives, the RNLI sent two lifeboats to Flamborough. If fishing boats were launching whatever the weather, so, too, should lifeboats and stations were established at both the North and South Landings.

Over the next sixty-three years, the pulling and sailing lifeboats at Flamborough recorded

Previous spread and above:
Numerous launchers are required to
recover the new Liverpool class
lifeboat at Flamborough, as she
returns from her first rescue mission
to two fishing cobles.

The North Landing and lifeboat
station at Flamborough, in the 1930s.

144 launches on service and saved the lives of 183 people. Once, in 1915, the entire 13-man crew of the No. 2 (South Landing) lifeboat survived a capsize in a whole gale and heavy seas while on service. They were all able to regain their self-righting boat and reach safety.

Eventually, in 1934, it was Flamborough's turn to be allocated a motor lifeboat. On a warm summer's day of that year the 35ft, single-engine Liverpool-type, *Elizabeth and Albina Whitley*, was officially named and launched down the precipitous slipway of the North Landing, over skids held steady by steely-nerved launchers on the beach and into the narrow inlet of sea.

It would be a while, however, before the advantages of motor power over oar and sail could be proved on a real service but, finally, on the morning of 4 January 1935, a call came for a Flamborough lifeboat. Two of the local motor fishing cobles, *Quest* and *Imperialist*, had been caught out at sea when a northerly gale blew up and there was considerable concern for them in the heavy breaking seas. In spite of the wind direction, the station honorary secretary John Bayes agreed with his coxswain George Leng that the new motor lifeboat should be launched rather than the pulling and sailing No. 2 boat, *Jane Hannah Macdonald*, at South Landing.

It was not an easy launch with large, angry waves surging in between the high white cliffs that guard either side of the landing place. The lifeboat needed some skilful coaxing from her coxswain in the surf before her propeller was sufficiently submerged to push her away from the shore. Once she was properly afloat, launchers on the shore stood and watched the new lifeboat heading out into the open sea, with waves breaking high over her and they knew that no pulling boat would have made it to sea in those conditions.

The lifeboat met the *Quest* about 2 miles out and escorted her back to the North Landing. She then put out again and found the *Imperialist* 4 miles to the north-east. On the coxswain's advice, the coble cut away her gear and the two vessels sailed in company to the shelter of Bridlington Bay. Her first mission accomplished, at about 2 p.m. the lifeboat returned to her station, where eager launchers were waiting to recover her on the beach.

The South Landing where today's Atlantic 75 lifeboat is launched.

According to a report of this service in the *Hull Daily Mail*, a local fisherman divulged: 'This is the first service launch of the new boat and apparently she is not quite right yet. It is a good job there was a flowing tide running, or there would have been serious trouble for the cobles and the lifeboat.'

Any suspicions that still existed about the performance of modern lifeboats were quickly dispelled. Calls on the old pulling lifeboat at the South Landing dried up completely and the boat was withdrawn in 1938. Meanwhile, the *Elizabeth and Albina Whitley* answered fifty-six calls and saved sixty-three lives in the fourteen years she served the station.

The lifeboat based at Flamborough nowadays is a 30-knot, rigid-inflatable Atlantic 75. However, she is stationed at the South Landing, as it is a more suitable site from which to launch and recover this type of boat.

16 Women Launchers

Cresswell and Hauxley, 1935

The popular Victorian image of a lifeboatman's frail wife, anxiously waving farewell from the doorway of her cottage, children clinging to her skirts, husband heading grimly for the boat-house, was often a far cry from the gritty reality of earning a living from the sea.

Small coastal communities relied as much on the women as the men to launch and recover the fishing boats and to deal with whatever catch was brought ashore. The weather may have been worse and the boat a bit heavier when it came to a lifeboat shout, but the womenfolk would still be there to get the boat away.

Previous spread: The lifeboat is hauled ashore at Hauxley, a small Northumberland fishing community. The station was open from 1852 to 1939 during which time the lifeboat was launched on 81 occasions and saved 246 lives.

Right: The women of Cresswell, Northumberland, were as vital as the men in getting the lifeboat to sea and safely back ashore.

Below: The legendary Margaret Armstrong of Cresswell in 1921, still pulling her weight at the age of seventy. She never missed a launch in fifty years.

Northumberland had by no means the monopoly on women lifeboat launchers; the female side of the Tart and Oiller families, for instance, living on the remote shingle headland of Dungeness in Kent would have been a tug-of-war match for any of their north-eastern counterparts. However, it was Northumberland villages such as Boulmer, Hauxley, Cresswell and Newbiggin where the women's physical involvement was perhaps most concentrated.

It is probably no more than a coincidence that one of the most famous women in the history of sea rescue, Grace Darling, came from one such community, Bamburgh, and performed her daring feat among the Farne Islands that lie just off that coast. However, when she and her lighthouse-keeper father launched their coble in 1833 to aid the men from the *Forfarshire*, the fact that she was a woman was of little significance to either of them; lives needed to be saved.

One Cresswell woman, Margaret Armstrong, was often referred to as 'the second Grace Darling'. In 1921, at the age of seventy, she was awarded a gold brooch by the RNLI in recognition of her assistance at every launch of the lifeboat for more than half a century. In that time she saw her father and three brothers lost together aboard their fishing boat and, later on, her son was drowned in similar circumstances.

When she was in her early twenties, in January 1876, a Swedish ship went aground near Newbiggin. As the tide prevented the lifeboat from getting near, Margaret and other women formed a human chain to try to reach the wreck. When this failed, she and two others were sent, through a blizzard, to Newbiggin to ask the coastguard to send the shore rescue apparatus.

The other two women were forced back by the elements but Margaret made it through, her feet bleeding, almost speechless with exhaustion. The equipment had been taken to Cresswell but by that time the lifeboat had managed to get alongside and completed the rescue.

Cresswell men had an alternative means of earning a living in the local coal mines. This meant that if the fishermen were at sea, there were still miners available to man the lifeboat. In November 1931, they were called into service

when cobles were caught out in a gale and put up distress signals. Women whose husbands were out in the gale went into the water up to their necks to get the lifeboat, *Martha*, away, and three of them had to be dragged back to safety through the surf. The lifeboat successfully shepherded all the cobles back to shore.

The two photographs of lifeboat recovery on the beach at Hauxley and Cresswell were taken in 1935, towards the very end of the era of women launchers. Watertight tractors were increasingly in use around the coast, their power essential to move the heavier motor lifeboats. Neither Cresswell nor Hauxley ever saw motor power. Both stations closed during the Second World War when their neighbours at Newbiggin and Amble were equipped with motor lifeboats.

Top: A 1926 crew and committee team at Hauxley with their Rubie type self-righting lifeboat, *Mary Andrew*.
Above: Cresswell in the 1930s with the lifeboat station in the foreground.

17 On the Cornish Rocks

The US cargo ship *Bessemer City* breaks in two, 2 November 1936

It would still have been dark when Henry Hocking, then aged ten, awoke early on a Monday morning in November, listening for the familiar sounds of the Trevega farmhouse routine which would already have been audible. That morning, though, something was different.

When he came downstairs, Henry was dismayed to discover that he had been allowed to sleep through the extraordinary events of the previous night, all of which had taken place barely half a mile from where he lay. An American cargo ship with thirty-three men on board had run on to the rocks at the bottom of the cliffs where his father's land met the Atlantic Ocean, just to the west of Pen Enys Point. Henry, desperate at least to be one of the first to see the wreck in daylight, begged for, and won, parental permission to be late for school that morning and bounded off across the fields towards the sea.

A great reader, his father had been up late the night before, sitting beside the kitchen stove, finishing a chapter of his book. A misty drizzle hung around the hills outside and a chill north-north-easterly wind was blowing straight off the sea. Suddenly he was conscious of a noise which he had never heard before coming out of the darkness. He opened the back door and listened. It was the reverberating sound of metal in torment and reminded him of a galvanised roof being torn from its rafters. It seemed to be coming from the sea.

Donning boots, coat and hat, he hurried along the track to the Eddy family at the next-door Trevalgan Farm to see what they made of it. There he discovered that his neighbour had already left the house to investigate what the racket was as it was disturbing his cattle. Soon Mr Eddy was back again and grabbing the telephone. The sound had led him to the cliff edge where he immediately saw below him the lights of a large ship, groaning as she slowly heaved herself backwards and forwards on the rocks beneath her hull. St Ives coastguard was alerted.

The town of St Ives was rudely woken, first by a rocket summoning the lifesaving apparatus team, then by the boom of the lifeboat maroon, which sounded just as the church clock struck midnight. The shore rescue team set off by road in the company of St Ives motor ambulance (in the charge of the aptly named Superintendent

Opposite: The wrecked American steamer, *Bessemer City*, a week after she ran aground near St Ives and broke in half.

Henry Hocking in the farmhouse kitchen where, when Henry was ten years old, his father had heard the sound of a ship grinding on the rocks. (*Edward Wake-Walker*)

Coxswain Tommy Cocking of St Ives. He was forced to board the *Bessemer City* himself to persuade her captain to abandon his vessel.

the crews might have had about relying on the internal combustion engine rather than their own muscle power had long since dissipated. The lifeboat had been brought to the station by sea from Cowes, successfully weathering a 70mph gale on the way and she had two good rescues under her belt already.

The stricken ship was not difficult to locate, hard up against the cliff. By now the lifeboat crew knew she was the *Bessemer City*, a 5,600-ton general cargo vessel bound from Liverpool to London, having begun her voyage in California. She belonged to the Isthmian Steamship Company and was carrying crates of tinned food. They presumed she must have misjudged her course while attempting to round Land's End and now was held against the rocks by a strong wind.

With great skill, Coxswain Cocking manoeuvred his lifeboat through the shallow, confused waters close in under the cliff and nudged up alongside the cargo vessel. He held his

W.H. Care), while crew and launchers began to assemble at the lifeboat house.

There was an exceptionally low spring tide that night and Tommy Cocking, the same coxswain who had launched in a gale to the *Sarah Evans* four years earlier (see Chapter 11), knew that it would be a real effort getting the lifeboat to sea. The water had retreated far beyond the harbour entrance and launchers had to drag the lifeboat on its carriage along the harbour road and then over more than half a mile of sand. The men at the end of the rope then steeled themselves for the icy cold sea as they pulled the carriage deeper and deeper into the water until they were up to their necks.

It may have been late on a Sunday night, but by now a considerable crowd had gathered along the west pier and when the lifeboat finally slipped off her carriage into the sea, a cheer rang out from the pier. The coxswain allowed himself a brief smirk; 15 minutes from callout to launch with that tide was not a bad effort by all concerned.

The lifeboat under his command was the 36ft, self-righting, motor-driven *Caroline Parsons*, which had replaced the pulling and sailing *James Stevens No. 10* three years earlier. Any misgivings

Carn Naun Point with the rocks on
which the *Bessemer City* foundered
in the foreground.
(*Edward Wake-Walker*)

The Hockings' Trevega Farm.
(*Edward Wake-Walker*)

position there while ten men clambered down a ladder over the ship's side and were bundled aboard the lifeboat. It was clear, though, that no general order to abandon ship had yet been given. The men who had come off were those not essential for saving the ship. Twenty-three remained on board.

The lifeboat pulled away from the *Bessemer City* and headed back to St Ives to land her evacuees. Just over an hour later she was back alongside the freighter. The tide was rising fast and she was in a worse position than before, pushed high up an unforgiving ridge of rock

which jutted out from the cliff. This time seventeen men were allowed to leave and, once again, the lifeboat made the 2½-mile passage back to St Ives with them.

The coxswain was now growing increasingly concerned for the safety of the *Bessemer City*'s captain and the five men still with him. He also knew that wind and tide were making each run in alongside that much more perilous for his boat and crew. Sure enough, when he drew close for a third time, a pungent smell of crude oil hung in the air and the surface of the water was black with the contents of the ship's ruptured fuel tanks. Now the lifeboat crew could see that the bow and stern of the vessel were moving independently of each other; she had broken in two amidships, as though cut by a knife.

There was no time to lose. With the ship in halves there was the imminent danger of the lifeboat being crushed as she lay alongside. But no one appeared in the least bit willing to come off. Eventually, the remaining five crewmen were coaxed down the side and into the lifeboat, but there was no sign of their captain. In desperation, Tommy Cocking himself jumped on to the ladder and hauled himself aboard the casualty. He had been told the captain was in his cabin and when he got there, he found the door locked and the captain inside. Fortunately, the Cornishman's considerable powers of persuasion won the day and the captain emerged and was hastened up on deck to the boarding ladder.

It was very nearly 7 a.m. when the lifeboat returned to her station with the last survivors. She was not a pretty sight, covered from stem to stern with thick black oil. It would be a nightmare cleaning job for her mechanic and his volunteer assistants.

The American crew of the *Bessemer City* received warm hospitality from the St Ives branch of the Shipwrecked Mariners' Society, all being found comfortable accommodation until they were able to return to the USA. The captain, A. Herman, could not enjoy the situation much. He told the local *St Ives Times* journalist that he preferred to say nothing about the incident but added: 'All I can say is, I had one ship, now I have two.'

When young Henry Hocking arrived at the scene, at first the abandoned ship appeared to be whole, until he looked more carefully and saw amidships a narrow slit of daylight which ran vertically, right through the hull. Over the next few days, this exotic, broken visitor became a source of grim fascination for him and hundreds more in the neighbourhood. A series of gales soon prised the two halves apart and the cargo spilled from the holds. Still apparently in very good condition, it was washed up for several miles along the coast, as far along as Porthmeor Beach at St Ives.

A more nutritious version of the *Whisky Galore* story cannot be imagined with store-cupboards in every local household groaning under the weight of tinned fruit and fish. Henry Hocking's only complaint was that all the labels had been washed off the tins, so no one knew whether it would be Pacific salmon or California peaches on the menu from one day to the next.

18 Ashore on the Gower Coast

The trawler *Roche Castle*, 10 January 1937

Eleven men aboard the steam-driven trawler *Roche Castle* were thankful this was their last night at sea and were looking forward to their own beds ashore after they had docked with the tide the following morning at Swansea. The hold was full of fish but January was the worst time to be catching them and every man aboard felt that on this trip, especially, he had earned his keep.

Skipper James Insole's familiarity with the Bristol Channel and its massive tides bred anything but contempt. Tonight, in particular, he was paying utmost respect. There was a heavy swell and a thick drizzling rain obscured all landmarks and lights. The trawler nosed her way up the Channel at no more than half speed, but her captain had misjudged his position and the course he had set would only lead to disaster.

Wireless operator John Horrington was down below in his bunk when he was suddenly shaken by a series of jarring bumps and the ghastly sound of solid rock grating along the hull. He rushed up on deck to find the skipper ordering his men to put out the fore and aft anchors while others prepared to launch the ship's boat. Seeing him, the skipper told him tersely to send out an SOS, which he did immediately and was relieved to get an instant answer that help was on its way.

The trawler had come to grief on a fatal strip of rock under Paviland Cliffs, not far from the village of Overton on the Gower peninsula. If her course had been only a degree or more to the south-east, she would have sailed past Porteynon Point and been safe. As it was, her troubles were worsening. The powerful surf which was breaking over her had smashed the wooden ship's boat to pieces against the rocks and any chance her crew had of hauling themselves off the rock by use of the anchors looked extremely slim.

There was no shortage of proffered help that night. One of the first to respond to the SOS was the Swansea ship, *Powis Castle*, which had been nearby. Her captain, Harry Batchelor, manoeuvred as close as he could and tried to land wires on board to pull the trawler off, but to no avail. Two other trawlers also came to stand by the wreck while attempts were made to refloat her.

The crew of The Mumbles motor lifeboat, *Edward, Prince of Wales*, felt a sense of *déjà vu*

Opposite: The battered remains of the steam trawler, *Roche Castle*, which ran on to the rocks near Overton on the Gower peninsula.

To effect communication with a vessel in distress the rocket (a) carrying the line (b) is fired over the vessel. The crew of the vessel by means of this line haul out the endless whip (c) and secure the whip block (d) to a mast or other suitable fixture on the vessel. This enables those on shore to haul out the hawser (e) to the vessel, where it is secured above the whip block. The hawser is then set taut through the block on the triangle (f) by means of the luff tackle (g). The breeches buoy (h) and endless whip are then secured to a traveller block on the hawser and those on shore haul the buoy to and from the vessel as often as may be necessary.

The rocket and breeches buoy equipment issued by the Board of Trade to volunteer lifesaving companies around the coast.

as they rounded Porteynon Point and saw the red flare put up by the *Roche Castle* to mark her position. Just over three years earlier they had launched to the Manx steamship *Ben Blanche* which had hit the self-same rocks in fog on her way into Swansea with a cargo of potatoes. On that occasion her crew had taken to their boats and the lifeboat had picked them up, when they were lost in the fog and not daring to attempt a landing on the jagged foreshore.

No ship, including the *Ben Blanche*, had been known to get away from this vicious spot. A rusty boiler, the only relic from the steamship, was spotted lying among the rocks about 150yds from the *Roche Castle* and the lifeboat crew were pretty sure that she would become yet another victim. With every wave that hit her, another wound was gouged into her steel plates as she rolled and thumped against the rocks. One thing was certain: it would be suicide for a lifeboat to run down into the surf and shallows to get alongside. All that her

coxswain could do was to stand off and watch what the trawler's skipper would do next.

The skipper was not going to give up his ship without a fight, even if he now had the means of escape, thanks to the dogged determination of the men of the Rhossili lifesaving company. When the alarm was raised, they had set off immediately into the wet night with their apparatus loaded on to a motor lorry. However, the position of the trawler meant that for the last mile, the apparatus had had to be carried as the men slid and sank sometimes up to their knees in agricultural mud and slime.

As they were setting up the equipment, about 150yds from the wreck, they were joined by Commander Hurst, their coastguard superior, based at The Mumbles. It took them a few shots, but by 11.30 p.m., a line was secured between the shore and the casualty. To their astonishment, no one aboard the trawler then showed any inclination to use it.

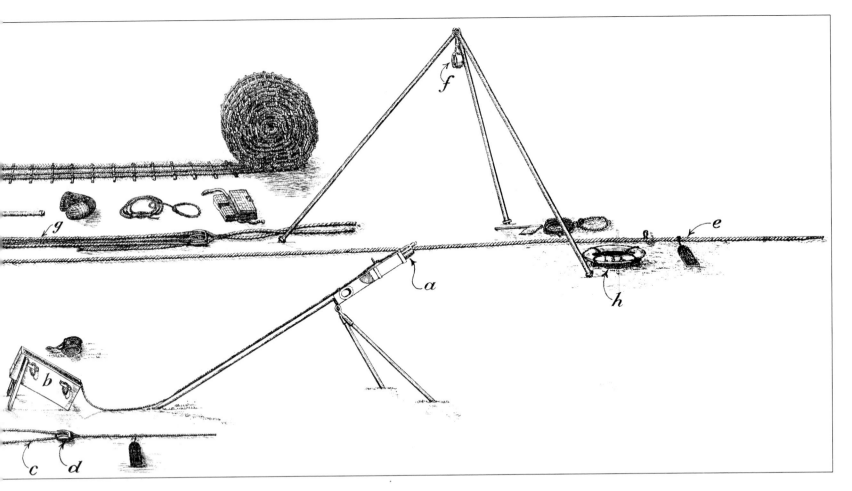

The Mumbles lifeboat station attached to the pier.

93

No ship had been known to get away from the vicious rocks which the *Roche Castle* struck on the night of 10 January 1937. (*Edward Wake-Walker*)

Instead, the crew kept working feverishly on the deck to try to free their vessel. Perhaps the captain thought that with the rising tide, there was still a chance of getting her afloat. But the rescue party ashore knew that a breeches buoy rescue was becoming more perilous with every inch the sea came in. With the vessel comparatively steady on the rock, the line would stay taut, but the more she moved with the sea, the less control they had over the fate of a man on the line.

Commander Hurst's concern and frustration rose with the tide. Now huge waves were picking up the trawler and dropping her back on the rocks with a sickening thud and grinding sound as she heeled first one way, then the next. Then an exceptionally powerful breaker caught her and deposited her broadside on to the cliff. The next breaker, larger still, washed over her and as it drained reluctantly from her decks, the men ashore

could just make out a shout from the skipper far below them: 'Hold tight! We are leaving.'

It was two and a half hours since the breeches buoy had first been rigged. Captain Insole had climbed 25ft up the rigging to direct the evacuation of his vessel, but even there, waves were constantly breaking over him. Maybe they did not hear his bellowed instructions that only one man at a time should get in the breeches buoy; maybe one or two crew members felt they had waited long enough. Whatever the case, the first two men to go, deckhand Thomas Baker and fireman George Gaylor, clambered in together clinging in a totally unconventional manner to the buoy.

Just as the men ashore had feared, the line could not be kept tight while they were being hauled across. Suddenly the line snapped taut and George Gaylor was catapulted into the sea. The shore crew continued to haul on the line as the

other man was still caught in the buoy by his foot. Somehow he was brought ashore, but received a battering on the rocks as he was pulled clear.

Pointing desperately at the water where his shipmate had disappeared, Baker was wrapped in a blanket and bundled away from the edge of the cliff. No one said anything, but they knew George Gaylor would not be seen alive again. There were still nine men alive aboard the trawler and they had to get them ashore. The breeches buoy was worked back and forth, each time returning with another drenched and shaken survivor.

The captain waited until his last man, John Horrington, the wireless operator, was safe before he descended from his perch and abandoned ship. The operation had taken 45 minutes and all that now remained was a desultory search for a man's body in the sea that would continue long into the next day.

The *Roche Castle*, damaged beyond redemption, continued the plaything of the waves at every high tide until no trace of her remained. The photograph here was taken several days after her grounding when only her bow portion was recognisable.

HM Coastguard continued to use rescue rockets until the 1980s, when they were superseded by helicopters for rescue close to the shore. (*Maritime and Coastguard Agency*)

19 Filming Henry Blogg

29 August 1937

There is something remarkably relaxed about Coxswain Henry Blogg's pose as he leans on a collecting box to face the cine camera of the man from Pathé News. True, there was no accompanying microphone in those days, so he had no fear of saying the wrong thing to the nation. It was not every lifeboat crew, however, whose faces were about to be shown in cinemas across the land, so you might have expected an element of awkwardness in their demeanour.

But this was the Cromer lifeboat crew and they were long accustomed to cameras and the press. When this photograph was taken, Henry Blogg had already won two Gold and two Silver Medals for gallantry and was famous as the most decorated serving lifeboatman. By the end of his 53-year career in 1947, he had broken every record in RNLI history, having been out on service 387 times saving 873 lives and winning three Gold and four Silver Medals in the process.

On this occasion, the crew were gathered outside the boathouse on the end of Cromer pier in readiness for the official naming of the station's two motor lifeboats, the larger twin-engined, Watson cabin class *H.F. Bailey*, launched from the pier, and the lighter Liverpool class *Harriot Dixon*, housed on the sea-front and launched from the beach off a carriage. The naming of both boats was somewhat overdue, the Watson having already been in service for two years and the Liverpool for three.

The *H.F. Bailey* was the second lifeboat at Cromer to bear the name of a London merchant who, in 1916, had left £10,000 to the RNLI in his will. The first *H.F. Bailey*, on station from 1923 to 1935, was the boat Blogg had used to take the two men off the *Sepoy* in 1933 (see Chapter 13). Aboard the second *H.F. Bailey* he would go on to win the Silver Medal in 1939 and the Gold and another Silver in 1941.

Mr Bailey's legacy did not quite cover the cost of both the boats named after him, so certain items aboard the second *H.F. Bailey* were allocated to other donors. Her searchlight, for instance, was funded by schools in Mitcham, Surrey, and her compass was paid for by RNLI supporters in Warsaw, Poland, proving just how far the Institution's reputation had spread, even in those uncertain, pre-war days.

The *Harriot Dixon* was the result of another legacy, this time from a Worthing surgeon, William Dixon, in memory of his mother. Had he or Mr Bailey still been alive, they would surely have been impressed to see who had been invited to perform the naming of the boats on their behalf. It was none other than the Home Secretary of the day, the Right Hon. Sir Samuel Hoare Bt, PC, GCSI, GBE, CMG, MP.

Opposite: Coxswain Henry Blogg and his crew pose for Pathé newsreel footage at the naming of their two new lifeboats in 1937.

Aerial shot of Cromer pier in the 1930s with the lifeboat station at its end.

The Cromer lifeboatmen who feature in this photograph are as follows (standing, left to right): Bob Davies, who took command of the pulling lifeboat in the *Sepoy* rescue (see Chapter 13); Walter Allen, who would later die of heart failure after having been washed out of the lifeboat with four others while on service to the *English Trader* in 1941; Coxswain Henry Blogg; Henry T. 'Shrimp' Davies, later to become coxswain at Cromer; Motor Mechanic Henry W. 'Swank' Davies and, kneeling, Louis Harrison, who, along with Walter Allen and Henry W. Davies, had been aboard the *H.F. Bailey* with Henry Blogg during the *Sepoy* rescue.

The first *H.F. Bailey* lifeboat stationed at Cromer.

Today's Tyne class lifeboats, *Ruby and Arthur Reed II*, launches from her slipway at the end of Cromer pier.

20 St Ives Lifeboat Overturns

With the crew of the wrecked steamer *Alba*, 31 January 1938

Nowadays, when a lifeboat crew performs a service to a vessel in trouble, the action is usually some miles out to sea and dramatic events are therefore seldom witnessed by anyone other than the rescuers and survivors themselves. Modern communications and fast lifeboats often allow serious trouble to be averted before a casualty gets close to shore.

The pages of this book show that the opposite was true in the first half of the twentieth century. In those days people seldom knew of a ship's distress until she had come ashore. Onlookers could be on the scene long before the lifeboat even arrived and the drama of a rescue would be played out before an audience of hundreds, occasionally thousands. On the night of 31 January 1938, the crowd of people who had rushed down to Porthmeor Beach in St Ives to see a steamer aground on the rocks were unaware that soon they would become participants in a rescue, not merely spectators.

The waters off Land's End in a west-north-westerly January gale and blinding rain could not have provided a more hostile and foreign environment for the SS *Alba* and her cosmopolitan crew as they battled south-westward through towering Atlantic seas. The 4,000-ton *Alba* had been built in the USA, originally for use on the Great Lakes. Then, after being laid up for some years, she had been bought by a Genoese company for ocean-going trade and was now taking a cargo of coal from Barry Dock, South Wales, to Civita Vecchia in Italy. Her captain, Yuluis Horvath, was one of fourteen Hungarians on board, the remaining nine men coming variously from either Yugoslavia, Romania, Spain, Portugal or Italy.

As he approached the Isles of Scilly, the captain realised that he would have to make a decision: carry on or turn back. His first engineer was not happy with the way the machinery was behaving and there was no sign of a let-up in the weather. He consulted his charts and made up his mind that he had to find shelter. The nearest would be behind the headland at St Ives, but it would not be easy to locate in the constant rain squalls and failing light.

The captain was relieved to see Godrevy Light, if only fleetingly, marking the eastward end of St Ives Bay, and he took a bearing. Then, for a second, he saw what he took to be the welcoming lights of St Ives itself and he turned the steamer head to wind and ordered the anchor to be let go.

Opposite: The Italian steamer, *Alba*, still pounded by heavy seas the morning after she ran aground on St Ives Head. Conditions had been much worse the night before when the St Ives lifeboat ran along her leeward side to take off her crew of twenty-three.

St Ives with Porthmeor Beach in the foreground and the rocks of St Ives Head, where the *Alba* struck, at its far end.

Even as he did so he was concerned at how little shelter the mooring seemed to offer. The mist and rain had come down thickly again, lights from the shore were no longer visible and large seas were crashing over the ship's bow.

What he did not realise was that he had dropped his anchor too soon, before rounding St Ives Head and was lying in a hopelessly exposed position off Porthmeor Beach. The lights he had glimpsed had not been harbour lights, but those from the outlying houses which line Porthmeor to the west of the Head. It was a fatal mistake; before the *Alba*'s cable held, her stern had struck rock and she was firmly aground.

Just after 7 p.m. Tommy Cocking, the veteran coxswain of the St Ives lifeboat, heard from his house in Virgin Street the long, urgent blasts of a steamer's siren and knew instantly that something was seriously amiss. Minutes later his fears were confirmed by a fisherman who told him that a ship was ashore to the west of St Ives Head. He wasted no time in reaching the lifeboat station and immediately fired a maroon to summon his crew and to let the casualty know that help was on its way.

That loud explosion was shortly followed by another, detonated by the coastguard whose local officers had picked up a radioed SOS, been astonished to discover a ship aground on the rocks immediately beneath their station and called for the life-saving appliances to be brought out.

Meanwhile, more than a hundred people had gathered at the lifeboat station to help with the launch, which was successfully accomplished within 15 minutes of the summons. In another 15 minutes, the 35ft 6in self-righter, *Caroline Parsons*, had fought her way around St Ives Head and was heading close inshore towards the steamer. Her coxswain and eight-man crew – including Tommy's sons Jack, the acting mechanic, and Tommy jnr – made out the *Alba*'s dark shape lying almost head to wind but with heavy seas crashing against her starboard side. The only chance of an approach meant going round the ship's bow to the sheltered port side. Crew members unlashed the anchor and, on the order, let it go, ahead of the steamer. The lifeboat then dropped down alongside her, nearly amidships.

Here the lifeboat lay, fairly comfortably, although 40ft seas, breaking right over the steamer, crashed down on to the lifeboat, knocking the breath out of her crew. They all looked up, shielding their faces with their hands, expecting to see men ready to board the lifeboat. Time was precious; the tide was ebbing and the seas were getting bigger and the line of breakers was coming closer and closer to where they lay.

To his amazement, the coxswain saw men attempting to lower their sea trunks and other baggage into the lifeboat. Waving it aside, he bellowed at the merchant crew to forget their belongings and to leave their vessel at once. There was clearly puzzlement aboard the *Alba* at the coxswain's urgent gesticulation and it was another 5 minutes before the first man stepped tentatively on to the ladder slung over the side of the ship.

Slowly others followed, apparently not understanding repeated entreaties to hurry. At last, only one man remained aboard, the second engineer who had gone back to the engine room to do something to protect his boilers. The lifeboat crew waited and waited, Tommy Cocking trying to explain in his plainest English to the captain the extreme dangers the delay was creating. Just as he had made the agonising decision to pull away, leaving the man on board, his head appeared over the rail and he clambered into the lifeboat. She had been alongside for forty crucial minutes.

This, the coxswain knew, was to be the most dangerous moment of all. As soon as he was clear of the side of the ship he would meet the full force of the massive breaking seas, arching their backs like a pack of snarling, slavering wolves, and preparing to envelop the lifeboat as she emerged. The plan was to hove on the anchor to bring the bow round so that the lifeboat could meet the seas head-on. But the anchor would not hold in the loose, sandy bottom which was being churned up by the crashing surf.

Now, once the anchor had been got aboard and stowed, the lifeboat would have to go astern into the breakers before she could be turned head to the seas; there was not enough room between the wreck and the rocks to turn her in the sheltered water. First, the coxswain ordered all the rescued men to lie down in the bottom of the boat to reduce top weight as much as possible. Then he went astern but would not have seen a monster breaker bearing down on the lifeboat and which came down on her like a moving wall. She was hit broadside on and rolled upside-down.

When the lifeboat righted herself seconds later, twenty-nine men were out of the boat, spluttering and struggling in the surf. Only three were still on board. Jack Cocking had clung to the engine control wheel in the shelter, Matthew Barber, the bowman, had been wedged among coils of cable and his brother William, in the stern, had kept firm hold of the starboard fore-and-aft line which he had been securing when the boat went over.

Coxswain Tommy Cocking, sixty-three years old, was thrown several yards from the boat. In fact, the shore and safety were not far away but, instead, he chose to swim back to the lifeboat. He explained: 'I said to myself, keep a cool head. By waiting, the sea brought me nearer the lifeboat and I was able to swim to her, being hauled aboard by my son.' His other son, Tommy jnr, recalled:

When the lifeboat capsized, I was thrown into the raging sea. I had heavy sea boots on and soon found these to be a great handicap, despite the fact that I had a lifejacket on. By working my legs in position, I managed to rid myself of the boots and stockings. By

Tommy Cocking jnr in 1978 when he was coxswain of the lifeboat. He, his brother Jack and his father Tommy were all on board the *Caroline Parsons* when she capsized after taking off the *Alba*'s crew.

St Ives lifeboat, *Caroline Parsons*, irreparably damaged on the rocks of St Ives Head.

this time the lifeboat righted herself and I swam to her and was pulled aboard.

The remaining four crew members also regained their lifeboat and all immediately set about pulling the men from the *Alba* out of the surf. They each had on a small kapok lifejacket and in a relatively short time eighteen of them were back in the lifeboat. Everyone on board scoured the sea for the remaining five while Jack Cocking worked desperately to restart the engine (it was designed to cut out on capsize so that the boat would not power away, out of control, with men in the water, once she had righted herself). To the mechanic's utter frustration, although the engine was undamaged, the starting handle had been struck by the mast during the capsize and was unusable. The lifeboat was therefore helpless.

On the shore, although it was dark and misty, the hundreds of people foregathered on Porthmeor Beach and St Ives Head had a pretty clear view of that night's events as they unfolded. Many were astonished at how close to the shore the lifeboat was operating. At the moment when the lifeboat rolled over and her white under-belly flashed into full view, a great gasp and cry of anguish echoed around the foreshore. Mothers, wives and sisters of the lifeboat crew covered their faces with their hands and then gazed aghast through their fingers as men's heads could be seen bobbing in the water around the boat.

The men of the lifesaving appliances company had reached the scene of the wreck just as the lifeboat had got alongside to take off the crew. Seeing the men boarding the lifeboat, they realised a rocket line was not needed and could, indeed, have endangered the operation if fired at that time. However, as soon as the lifeboat capsized, a line was fired across the *Alba*. They could see the crew scramble back on board and grab the line, thus preventing the lifeboat being carried away by the tide. Instead, the seas began to wash the lifeboat towards the rocks where the rocket men and spectators were standing. Men from the *Alba* could be seen preparing to leap from the lifeboat as she neared the rocks and the coxswain could be heard screaming at them to stay on board unless they wanted to be crushed between the lifeboat and the rocks.

People from the town were now beginning to scramble over the rocks towards the sea, joining members of the lifesaving company. Coastguards, police, sea scouts and ordinary citizens in their scores slithered, stumbled and fell across the jagged boulders to get close enough to the lifeboat to help people ashore. One man from the lifesaving company injured his shoulder as he was hurled against a rock by a wave while trying to get a line to the lifeboat. A colleague took over from him and succeeded in getting it aboard.

Now the coxswain was ready to let men ashore. With illumination from searchlights and car headlamps, rescuers grabbed at the sodden clothing of survivors and hauled them out of the sea. Many of the *Alba*'s men sustained severe cuts and bruising and her captain broke his leg. The lifeboat crew also abandoned their boat and were helped ashore, more or less unscathed.

Superintendent Care and his men of the St Ives Motor Ambulance, together with colleagues from Redruth and Camborne, were hard at work that night. There was nothing they could do, however, for the *Alba*'s first and second engineers or the mess boy whose badly battered bodies were washed ashore. They, along with the second officer and the steward, whose bodies were never found, were the five who failed to make it back to the lifeboat after the capsize.

The lifeboat, the *Caroline Parsons*, did not survive the night. Although virtually undamaged when she was abandoned, the gale and tides carried her over the rocks and she was a sorry sight, broken beyond repair when daylight came. At the express wish of the coxswain, crew and all the lifeboat station officials, the RNLI removed the engine and a number of reusable fittings and then set fire to the remains. This was preferable to her falling prey to souvenir hunters and remaining a forlorn, disintegrating memorial to the event.

The *Alba* was not so easily disposed of but she was slowly dismantled by salvage men, wind and weather. Even today, her boilers can be seen protruding from the sand when the tide is low.

At the inquest which followed two days later, a verdict of accidental death of the five *Alba* crew

members was recorded. The first officer, standing in for his injured captain, praised the handling of the lifeboat by coxswain and crew. Tommy Cocking, in turn, praised his lifeboat, dispelling any doubt there may have been that she was fit for the task. He said: 'It was one of the best engines ever put in a lifeboat and I am sorry to lose the boat, she was beautiful.'

One juror asked whether the lifeboat carried oars and was told that two pairs were on board but that they were unusable in those circumstances. Another juror questioned the arrangements for cooperation between coastguards and lifeboat station. He was assured that all rescue services worked closely together in St Ives and that it was only because the coxswain received news early about the wreck from a fisherman that he fired the maroon before hearing from the coastguard.

Of course, there would have been countless unofficial inquests in bars all around St Ives in the days which followed. What if the men had come off the steamer sooner? Conditions would not then have been so bad for the lifeboat's return. What if the men had stayed put and waited for the weather to improve? They would all have survived then. Why didn't the lifeboat wait until a rocket line and breeches buoy rescue had been attempted? The lifeboat would never have needed to work so perilously close to the shore.

The answer to each of these hypothetical questions is maybe, but the speculators were not the ones who had to make a decision amid the fury of the storm. All that Coxswain Cocking would have known was that he had the means to do something to save the men on the ship. Moreover, he was carrying the expectation of hundreds, if not thousands, of local spectators that he would get alongside and get the men off – which he did.

His bravery was recognised by the RNLI with the award of the Silver Medal; his crew all received the Bronze. The Mayor and inhabitants of St Ives collectively received the RNLI's official thanks inscribed on vellum for the heroic efforts of citizens in hauling men alive from the sea. In the week following the event, two BBC radio broadcasts were made. The first involved the coxswain and second coxswain travelling to Plymouth to give their account and the second was an appearance of the lifeboat signalman, John Thomas, on the BBC's *In Town Tonight*, broadcast from London.

21 Crippled in 108mph Winds

Fishing Boat and Schooner off New Brighton, 23 November 1938

Officials of today's New Brighton lifeboat station were recently surprised but delighted to come across an old diary which had been kept by one of their former coxswains, William 'Pinky' Jones, and which chronicled the seven years during which he had charge of the station's two lifeboats (one sailing, one motor), up to his retirement at the age of sixty-five in December 1938.

Occasionally he would record heated exchanges between himself and his apparently headstrong motor mechanic, Wilfred 'Wally' Garbutt, who sometimes seemed inclined to act without informing his coxswain, such as by launching a motor dinghy to an incident rather than calling out the lifeboat. Another tantalising entry states only: 'W. Liversage [a crew member] made insulting remarks about service to schooner, *Mimmie*.'

In the main, though, the diary is a briefly worded and unemotional record of everyday life at the station, with strict attention paid to the detail of who was on the crew at every launch and the amount of expenses due and paid to the men. He records a trip he made to the West

Country to sail a relief lifeboat back to the station and follows with proprietorial zeal the progress of the station's own lifeboat while she is undergoing a refit at a local yard.

His pride in the lifeboat was understandable; New Brighton, one of the few stations to operate a tubular oar-powered boat, then a steam-driven lifeboat both in the 1890s, was chosen by the RNLI in 1923 to pioneer the largest motor lifeboat ever built, the 60ft, twin-engined Barnett class. With the increased range offered by motor lifeboats, the RNLI was intending to build larger boats capable of surviving the worst of offshore conditions.

By 1938, three more 60ft Barnetts and a further ten 51ft versions had entered service and in September of that year, Coxswain Jones had the *William and Kate Johnston*, his own original version, back at her mooring after her three and a half month overhaul. He must have thought that a launch in October to rescue two men in a ship's lifeboat on a bank at the mouth of the Mersey would be his last before retirement.

But he had reckoned without the storm which sprang up in the early hours of Wednesday

Opposite: In spite of being badly damaged, New Brighton lifeboat, the *William and Kate Johnston*, returns to the landing stage with all the survivors from the fishing boat *Progress* and the schooner *Loch Ranza Castle*.

23 November and which, by the time it had swept across the country, had taken at least five lives on land and caused twenty-seven lifeboats to put out to the rescue around the coast. At New Brighton westerly winds of over 100mph were being recorded when, at about quarter past nine that morning, the ominous ring of the telephone could just be heard in the coxswain's house above the thunderous sound of hail and rain squalls beating against the roof and windows. A fishing boat had been reported drifting east-north-east of Crosby Lightship and seemed to be in serious trouble.

To follow what happened next purely in the understated words of Pinky Jones's diary would seriously risk obscuring the enormity of what he and his volunteer crew achieved that day. 'Winds west with very heavy seas' is the nearest he gets to hyperbole in his account, although he does note that throughout the lifeboat's mission her steering gear was inexplicably stiff, making his task considerably more difficult.

It took the lifeboat about 35 minutes to cover the 6½ miles to the position given by the lightship. As the lifeboat reared up on to the crest of a wave, crew members, fighting for their balance, peered through horizontal rain for a sight of a sail or a mast. The first vessel they saw was not a fishing boat but a two-masted schooner, her sails in tatters, waves breaking right over her and drifting very close to the shore off the town of Crosby.

Moments later, the fishing vessel was also in their sights, at anchor but floundering desperately amid towering seas, her sails completely blown away. Although she was in deeper water than the schooner, she was a much smaller vessel and Coxswain Jones made the difficult decision to attend to her first.

The looming outline of the New Brighton lifeboat was a sight for the sorest of eyes aboard the Hoylake fishing boat, *Progress*. The three young men on board had been out all night in the storm and were terrified. They watched as the lifeboat made two or three attempts to get alongside, her coxswain straining with all his strength at the unresponsive helm.

Before too long he had succeeded and the fishermen were able to leap from their vessel into the lifeboat. Immediately, the coxswain set course for the schooner. Behind them, the *Progress* had already disappeared beneath the waves. The weather continued to deteriorate and in the violent squalls and spindrift and spray it was all but impossible to see ahead.

The schooner in distress was the 74-ton *Loch Ranza Castle*, which had sailed from her home port of Annalong in Co. Down the day before with a cargo of kerb stones, bound for Canning Dock in Liverpool. Her skipper, William McKibbin, later explained:

> After facing heavy seas, which pitched our boat about like a cork for some hours, we found ourselves in trouble about 11 o'clock this morning. We lost our foresail and stay sail and the engine room became flooded with water. The masts remained intact.
>
> We put out a distress flag and this was evidently seen by the crew of the nearby Crosby Lightship. They flashed messages on our behalf by radio telephone. It was a frightening experience, for we had to cling to the rigging for at least half an hour. We were jolly thankful when we saw the *William and Kate Johnston* arrive on the scene.

In fact, knowing that there were now two vessels in trouble, the authorities had also called out Hoylake's motor lifeboat, *Oldham*, in support. Meanwhile, the New Brighton boat drew close to the schooner and her crew could begin to make out that she was right among the surf which was breaking about 250yds from the shore. As the lifeboat came closer still to take soundings, it was obvious that the ship had actually sunk and four dark specks could be seen in the rigging, two on the port and two on the starboard side.

The coxswain headed seaward again, let go an anchor and veered down towards the wreck, working his engines to keep the cable slack. The lifeboat was manoeuvred straight over the sunken vessel to get near to the starboard rigging. Once, during the repeated efforts to get close enough to reach the men, there was a sickening jolt as the lifeboat struck the submerged bulwark of the vessel hard with her bow. The coxswain was pretty certain that something had given aboard his boat. Eventually, though, the men on the starboard rigging were dragged aboard. Of the

Opposite: New Brighton had a history of trying out new lifeboat designs. From 1888 to 1898 the station operated a 'tubular' lifeboat (above), whose rowing platform was supported by two air-tight metal tubes; a precursor, perhaps, of the inflatable lifeboats of the present day. Then, between 1897 and 1923, the station took charge of a rare steam-driven lifeboat, *Queen* (below).

The *William and Kate Johnston.*
New Brighton was the first station to
operate a 60ft, twin-engine Barnett
class lifeboat.

men on the port side, one was seen to climb
further up and cross to the starboard rigging. The
other looked very groggy and, apart from
removing his sea boots, seemed unable to move.

The lifeboat came in again over the bulwarks
and her crew grabbed the man who had made it
to the starboard side. It was now clear that the
only way to get the last man off was somehow
to take the lifeboat around the port and
leeward side. The man, in his mid-sixties, had
apparently injured his head, his face was
bleeding and he looked ready to drop from his
perch at any moment.

It had taken a whole hour to get the first
three men off and by now not a single deck
fitting of the schooner was showing and the
lifeboat was being subjected to a bombardment
of blocks, yards and rigging torn from the
masts. The lifeboat drew clear to windward and,
as calmly and as quickly as they were able, the
crew bent a second anchor cable to the one by
which they were already anchored. Then the
coxswain veered down, stern first, passing under
the casualty's bowsprit and, keeping the
starboard engine slow ahead, got right alongside
the port rigging.

The man, in his semi-conscious state, now only knew to grasp the rigging. There were some very anxious moments as the crew fought to prise his hands away from the ropes. At last they had him on board and the second mechanic immediately began to administer first aid. The coxswain coaxed the lifeboat clear of the wreck, cut his cable and headed thankfully home. By now he was well aware that the lifeboat had indeed been damaged; the two forward compartments and the cabin were full of water and she was down nearly 3ft by the head.

As she got close to the landing stage at New Brighton, people ashore could see the propellers showing above the water and knew that the lifeboat had clearly been in the wars. The coxswain still had one final difficult manoeuvre to make; instead of picking up the mooring and taking his survivors ashore via the boarding boat, he wanted to get them ashore quickly by coming alongside the ferry landing stage. He was very worried about the health of the last man off. The picture shows how one false move by the coxswain could have been disastrous during this manoeuvre. As it was, he made it alongside and the survivors were put ashore.

The Hoylake lifeboat had made it through to the Crosby Channel just in time to be told that all were saved. Her coxswain could only swing his boat round and battle his way back against the storm, arriving at station an hour and a half later.

In his diary, the New Brighton coxswain records his visit to Cubbins boatyard in Birkenhead, two days after the rescue, to visit his damaged lifeboat. He is met by none other than the RNLI's Chief Inspector of Lifeboats, Commander Edward Drury, up from London, together with the Institution's Naval Architect, Richard Oakley (who would one day have a lifeboat design named after him). Together, they looked at the damage which consisted of a hole, 3ft × 3in, in the skin of the fore cabin and two slightly smaller holes in two other outer compartments. Half the bilge keel had been torn off on the starboard side and there was a considerable amount of other minor damage. A maladjusted bush in the gear had apparently caused the tight steering.

Any fears held by the coxswain of a reprimand were allayed by the Chief Inspector's congratulations on a very fine service, during which, he was told, he should have done more damage. In fact, two weeks later, he heard that he had been awarded the RNLI's Silver Medal for gallantry; his second coxswain, John Nicholson, and mechanic, Wilfred Garbutt, received Bronze Medals and the remaining four crew members the Institution's official thanks on vellum.

Sadly, this news arrived too late for one of the crew that day, J. Stonall. He had collapsed and died of heart failure on his boat while out fishing just four days after the rescue.

22 Disaster at St Ives

23 January 1939

It is six in the morning on Monday 23 January 1939 and there has been precious little sleep for either humans or animals at Godrevy Farm. All through the night an Atlantic gale of immense ferocity has launched assault after assault against the fabric of this bleak farmstead standing close to Godrevy Point at the eastern end of St Ives Bay. There is almost bound to be damage to repair by daybreak.

The doorbell rings and a man's intermittent shout can just be heard above the wind. No one usually calls at this time of day. Mrs Delbridge sends her husband downstairs to investigate. He opens the front door, sees nothing, then looks down to find what appears to be a dripping heap of tattered yellow oilskin. There is a slight movement and a white, battered face looks up at the farmer from the doorstep. 'St Ives lifeboat is wrecked,' it croaks, 'and I am the only survivor.'

The epic rescue of the crew of the *Alba* in January 1938 and the ensuing capsize of the lifeboat, *Caroline Parsons* (see Chapter 20), had caused extensive discussion in St Ives and at RNLI headquarters about what was an appropriate boat for this busy Cornish port. Although Coxswain Tommy Cocking was still

fulsome in his praise of the light (7-ton) self-righter which he had lost that night, even he agreed a bigger, heavier boat would be better for the sort of seas that he and his crew sometimes encountered.

The problem was that St Ives harbour dried out at low tide and the only way to guarantee a 24-hour service was to maintain a carriage-launching lifeboat of limited weight and dimensions. One idea was to keep a 45ft, 20-ton Watson cabin type moored permanently afloat off the old breakwater, but that had to be abandoned when the coxswain realised he would not be able to reach her by boarding boat in all weathers. For more than a century the town of St Ives had been petitioning the government to provide a break-water to give all-weather shelter, but with no success. Neither was there a suitable place anywhere nearby to build a slipway from which a larger lifeboat could be launched at all states of the tide.

Instead, a lifeboat very slightly broader in the beam and lower in the water than the *Caroline Parsons* had been ordered for St Ives and while she was being built, another light self-righter, *John and Sarah Eliza Stych*, no longer required at Padstow, was sent to St Ives as a stop-gap. Presumably, the fact that she was only a temporary replacement

The St Ives crew in 1937, two years before the disaster. The men (left to right) are: Jack Cocking, Richard Stevens, Second Coxswain William Peters, Coxswain Tommy Cocking, Matthew Barber and John Thomas. All but William Peters lost their lives aboard the lifeboat on the night of 23 January 1939. William Peters had been one of the crew to survive the capsize following the *Alba* service in 1938 (see Chapter 20).

allowed all concerned to accept that the ex-Padstow boat was a good ton lighter even than the *Caroline Parsons* and had 5in less beam.

Nevertheless, just before half past two in the morning of 23 January 1939, as the *John and Sarah Eliza Stych* stood on her carriage, poised to launch into the night, there were some very anxious faces surrounding her. Many were the same faces that had watched in horror a year earlier when the lifeboat was bundled over in the surf in full view of the town. Now, an identical lifeboat was to be launched, in conditions which were much worse

than those of a year ago, to an unidentified ship in distress off Cape Cornwall. That would mean an 11-mile passage against a gale which was already wrenching tiles from the roofs above their heads.

There had been a chance that the lifeboat would not be required. The honorary secretary and coxswain had waited to hear whether the Sennen Cove lifeboat could get away. She was nearer and up-weather of the ship in trouble and she was also a bigger boat. Unfortunately, the station could not launch for two hours either side of low water and the message soon came back that a launch was, indeed, impossible. At that, Tommy Cocking had announced, 'We are off', and sprang up to fire the maroon.

As the lifeboat was manhandled into position at the top of the ramp, Sergeant H. Osborne of the local police, who was among the launchers and who had overseen the rescue of the lifeboat crew when they were washed on to the rocks the previous year, wished the coxswain good luck. 'Thank you, sergeant', replied Cocking, 'we shall be all right.'

One woman in the gathering crowd, Margaret Freeman, was visibly distressed. Not only was her brother already aboard the boat, her 36-year-old fisherman husband William was now solemnly donning a lifejacket handed to him by the coxswain. He had only turned up to help with the launch. The last time he had been out in the lifeboat was more than six years ago when there was still a pulling and sailing boat at the station. What had now possessed him, she wondered desperately, to proffer himself when one of the regular crewmen had handed back his lifejacket at the last minute, apparently feeling unwell?

She watched helplessly as some ninety launchers hauled the lifeboat carriage across the sandy bottom of the harbour to where it met the breakers. In their attempt to get the lifeboat afloat, men were being swept off their feet in the surf and thrown hard against the carriage. Eventually they succeeded and the lifeboat headed for open sea, bucking and rolling violently even while still in the lee of St Ives Head.

Together with the coxswain on board that night were four other men who had survived the capsize of a year ago: his son Jack Cocking, the brothers Matthew and William Barber and John Thomas, the signalman. Mechanic Richard Stevens (the coxswain's son-in-law), Edgar Bassett, another last-minute stand-in, and William Freeman made up the rest of the crew.

And it was William Freeman who, in just over three hours' time, would be found utterly exhausted and traumatised on the doorstep of Godrevy Farm. The following day he had recovered sufficiently to give this account of his terrible experience which was published in the *St Ives Times* of 27 January 1939:

> We were all right until we were about a mile and a half from Clodgy Point. I was in the bows of the boat with William Barber and Edgar Bassett. The rest were aft. We were holding on to the lifelines, which are part of the boat's equipment.
>
> Suddenly an unexpected sea struck us on the starboard bow and the boat capsized instantly. There was no hesitation about it, she was no sooner hit than she was over. I was in the water before I knew what had happened. I retained hold of my lifeline, but the coxswain, William Barber, Edgar Bassett and John Thomas were thrown some distance from the lifeboat. When the boat righted itself Matthew Barber and Richard Stevens pulled me aboard.
>
> I heard John Thomas shouting. I got a torch and shone it in the direction of the voice but could see nothing. I never saw nor heard any more of those four.

The lonely Godrevy Farm where William Freeman found help. (*Edward Wake-Walker*)

115

William Freeman, seen through his window with his wife and mother, the day after the disaster. (*Pathé*)

All the ropes and gear were trailing over the side of the lifeboat. I got an axe and gave it to Stevens who set about cutting it away. When we thought all was clear we started up the engine. It started beautifully, but as soon as we let in the gear a rope flowing over the stern, which had been overlooked, jammed the propeller.

The only thing to do now was to drop anchor, which we did. We tried to put up the mizzen mast, but there was not enough of us now aboard to do it. Then we burnt red flares, and after they had burnt out we put up white ones. We saw a rocket fired from the coastguards, and we knew they must have seen us.

Just then the anchor rope broke, and we were once again at the mercy of the sea. Stevens started the engine again but the propeller jammed once more. This went on two or three times and while we were doing it, the boat capsized for the second time.

I was prepared for it this time. I jammed my wrist in a railing under the canopy and held on to the starting handle of the engine with my right hand. I found that the pressure of the air trapped under the canopy was sufficient to keep the water out, and even though I was standing upside-down, with the boat keel upwards, my face was not in water.

This time the boat came up again quicker, because she had no gear. Stevens was thrown clean away and we never saw him again.

There were now only three of us in the boat, Matthew Barber, Jack Cocking and myself. We knew then that the engine was useless and we could only drift. When we got close to Godrevy, Barber said: 'Well boys, we shall all go together.' I said: 'No, stick to her while she's afloat.' I had in mind the way she came ashore after the *Alba* wreck and I thought if we could hang on to her, we should be saved.

Then she capsized for the third time and Barber and Cocking were thrown out. I felt them go past me, but I never saw them again. I was left there by myself. Three minutes later the boat struck the rock. If Barber and Cocking could only have held on for that last short time they would have been saved.

The lifeboat was thrown upon the rocks on her port side, and the sea left her. I looked over the side and saw there was no water around. I simply walked out of her and scrambled over the rocks and up the cliffs.

First I found a small hut but that was locked. I walked around a bit and caught sight of a farmhouse. I went up to it and rang the bell and shouted. Mr and Mrs Delbridge took me in and gave me every care. They could not have done more for their own son.

I don't know that I shall ever be able to go to sea again as a fisherman. The shock has been terrific. Every time I think about it my body shivers from head to foot. I have received telegrams asking me to broadcast, but I can't do it. I couldn't do it knowing that my friends are still out there and others are being buried.

William Freeman never did set foot aboard a boat again and even a walk along the pier presented problems. He died on 23 January 1979, on the fortieth anniversary of his ordeal. The bodies of the coxswain and his son and the Barber brothers came ashore almost immediately; the remaining three were recovered over the next fortnight.

It had been an anguished time for the people on shore waiting to discover what had become of the lifeboat after she had set off into the darkness at ten to three. The coastguard at Clodgy Point had, indeed, spotted the red flares put up after the first capsize at four twenty, their literal message being: 'More help needed'. What kind of help? Had they found the casualty? Were they in difficulty themselves? All the coastguard could do was to ask Penlee lifeboat to launch, but she was 30 miles away on the south coast of Cornwall. They also sent rocket lifesaving teams out to Godrevy and Portreath, the first places downwind of the signals where something would come ashore.

Otherwise, they just had to wait. Nothing more came from the lifeboat or from the ship that had signalled a distress. It was not until seven that William Freeman's terrible news reached St Ives. Farmer Delbridge had had to bicycle more than a mile to the nearest telephone to raise the alarm. When he arrived he discovered the gale had brought the lines down and he had to pedal another three miles into the wind to Hayle to find a phone that worked.

When search parties reached Godrevy Point they were astonished to find the lifeboat deposited on a plateau of ragged rock, several feet higher than the tide ever came. The power and the height of the waves which hurled her there must have been very great.

As for the anonymous distress call which caused this disaster, it remained a mystery until a young man's body and a broken lifebuoy were found washed up at Wicca Pool, west of St Ives, two days later. The lifebuoy bore the name: SS *Wilston*. Over the next few days, further wreckage came ashore and coal was found littered around the rocks. Eventually, more bodies were found and identified and the Glasgow owners of the *Wilston*, which had left Newport on 21 January with coal destined for the Mediterranean, were forced to accept that their ship had been wrecked with the loss of all

thirty-one hands. It had to be assumed that the SOS had come from her.

The devastation caused to the people of St Ives by the disaster was total. Every local family had some connection to the men who were lost from the lifeboat. Each left a widow and there were eight dependent children. The lifeboat station had lost its heart and soul and would remain closed for a year. The fishing community was in deep mourning and the local rugby club had lost a respected referee in John Thomas and two competent players in the Barber brothers.

The RNLI awarded its Bronze Medal to William Freeman and his seven fellow crewmen posthumously. Of Coxswain Thomas Cocking, *The Lifeboat* journal said in its official report:

> He was a coxswain of long experience, and all who knew him at St Ives described him as a natural leader, a man who did not know what fear was. No man, they said, could have stopped him taking his boat to sea, and his crew would follow him, as they did, to death.

The station reopened in 1940 after the disaster and since then it has seen two further Tommy Cockings as coxswain, son and grandson of the original. It still has a carriage-launched lifeboat, *The Princess Royal*, a 14-ton, all-weather Mersey class with twin 285hp engines, capable of 16 knots.

The present-day St Ives lifeboat, *The Princess Royal*. She is launched by tractor and carriage, has twin 285hp engines and is capable of 16 knots. (*Royal Bank of Scotland/Rick Tomlinson*)

23 Collision off Cromer

12 October 1939

For more than six months following the declaration of war on 3 September 1939, the people of Great Britain wondered what sort of war it was that they were engaged in, given the sparse evidence of hostilities at home or across the Channel. Those who spent their life at sea, on the other hand, were under no illusion whatsoever of a phoney war.

By the end of March 1940, just within the waters of the British Isles, enemy action had accounted for the loss of 38 Royal Navy vessels and 278 British and neutral countries' merchant ships. Already nearly three thousand men had lost their lives. Germany knew that she would greatly weaken her island enemy by making an early assault on its sea traffic and she did so with a combination of battleships, submarines, aircraft and mine-laying.

The North Sea was a major battlefield and east coast lifeboat stations very soon realised that they would be called on relentlessly to pick up the pieces. Only a week into the war, Aldeburgh lifeboat brought back seventy-four oil-blackened survivors from the Liverpool steamer, *Magdapur*, after she had hit a mine and broken her back off the Suffolk coast.

A month on from that incident and the 63-year-old coxswain Henry Blogg of Cromer had already earned his first Silver bravery medal of the Second World War.* The Greek steamer, *Mount Ida*, was not a direct victim of warfare but her demise on the Ower Bank, 32 miles east of Cromer in the early morning of 9 October 1939, would probably not have happened in peacetime. The ship had been at sea for fifty days and her

---

* He had previously won a Gold Medal for service to a ship blown in half by a mine during the First World War and another in 1927 after going to an oil tanker on Haisborough Sands. His third Gold Medal came in 1941 when he rescued eighty-eight seamen from six steamers in a convoy which ran on to Haisborough Sands. Blogg's three other Silver Medals were awarded in 1932, 1933 (see Chapter 13) and 1941.

Cromer's carriage-launched No. 2
lifeboat, the Liverpool class *Harriot
Dixon*, used by Henry Blogg to
rescue the crew of the *Linwood*.

Previous spread: The 1,500-ton
Linwood, victim of a collision, is
driven ashore by her skipper to save
his ship and her crew.

Cromer sea-front.

skipper became disoriented by a coastal blackout which deprived him of any guiding lights.

The steamer sprang a leak as heavy seas pounded her on the sands and her engine room was flooded. In a rescue at the very limit of his lifeboat's range, which Blogg later described as one of the hardest he had ever accomplished, he took off all twenty-nine aboard. Sadly, one of the Greek crew crushed his leg so badly while leaving the ship that he later died in Cromer Hospital.

No sooner had the *H.F. Bailey* landed the survivors than she was called to the aid of a Lowestoft drifter, ashore 7 miles along the coast. She stood by as the crew were rescued by breeches buoy. When they returned to station, Cromer lifeboat crew had been at sea for twenty hours.

Only two nights later they were again woken by a maroon. Arriving at the waterfront just before midnight, in pouring rain, they might have taken some ironic comfort from the fact that this time their casualty had come to them and was ashore only a mile south-east of Cromer.

She was the 992-ton steamship *Linwood* of Middlesbrough, in ballast, bound from Ipswich for Hartlepool. Her captain, I. Jones, had been in his bunk when the ship juddered horribly and lurched sideways from her course. As he rushed on deck he was convinced they had hit a mine. He soon discovered, though, that they had been struck on the starboard side by the bow of another vessel, which had loomed up out of the deluging rain. She was now out of sight again but could be heard blowing an SOS on her whistle, presumably on behalf of the vessel she had struck.*

The *Linwood* was now listing and she was starting to fill with water. With the safety of the crew his first priority, Captain Jones decided to steer immediately for the coast and run his ship ashore. The men could be got ashore and, if salvage were possible, that could come later. As soon as she was aground, flares were put up to guide rescuers to the ship.

This time Henry Blogg decided to take Cromer's No. 2 lifeboat, the carriage-launched Liverpool class, *Harriot Dixon*, to the rescue. She had a shallower draft than the *H.F. Bailey* and would therefore be easier to manoeuvre alongside the beached steamer.

By Blogg's standards, the ensuing rescue of the twelve men aboard in a moderate north-westerly wind and moderate sea conditions was nothing more than routine. The lifeboat launched at midnight, ran in alongside the *Linwood*, remained there long enough for the crew to be taken aboard, and was back on the beach with survivors before 1 a.m.

The *Linwood* was eventually salvaged although it was far from easy, the task being severely hampered by bad weather and gear failure. The operation took nearly a month, but finally, on 9 November, she was refloated and towed into Great Yarmouth by the tug *George Jewson*. Two weeks later she was able to resume her passage north to Hartlepool.

She was not destined to survive the war, however. Almost exactly three years later, on 15 November 1942, the *Linwood* struck a mine 2 miles south-east of the Long Sand Head Buoy in the Thames estuary. She sank in 34ft of water with the loss of three of her four passengers and three of her thirteen-man crew.

---

* The vessel to strike the *Linwood* was another steamer, the *Skipjack*, travelling south, bound for Gravesend. She stood by out of sight for a while, then continued her voyage to the Thames, relatively unaffected by the collision.

24 Wartime Convoy's Sick Man Saved

Walmer, Kent, 19 October 1939

Inevitably, Kentish lifeboat stations were more directly involved in the war effort than any others in the country. So much of the major conflict close to home happened in their neighbourhood and although the RNLI maintained its resolve to rescue people regardless of race, colour or creed, the lifeboats in the south-east were always likely to be viewed as an asset by the British military.

Pilots downed in the Battle of Britain and throughout the war often had a lifeboat crew to thank for their survival, and countless shipping casualties in the vicinity would have fared much worse without the RNLI to call upon.

When it came to the evacuation of Dunkirk in June 1940, the RNLI had agreed to the enlistment of no fewer than nineteen of its lifeboats from Sussex round to Norfolk in the operation. Most were commandeered by Royal Navy personnel and therefore many details of what they achieved were lost in the fog of war.

Walmer's twin-engined, Watson class *Charles Dibdin* (*Civil Service No. 2*), was one such lifeboat which, when she was eventually returned from the beaches, had holes in both sides and a tracer bullet embedded in one of her air-case compartments.

Seven months prior to her cross-Channel adventure, the Walmer lifeboat's coxswain, Joseph Mercer, and his crew were carrying out another kind of evacuation, if not before a hostile enemy, then certainly in hostile weather conditions and with a man's life saved as a result. First, on the evening of 18 October 1939, a doctor contacted the station to say that he had been asked by the senior naval officer at Ramsgate to go aboard a Dutch steamer, the *Mirza*, which was lying at anchor off the town with a number of other merchant vessels.* There was a gale blowing and a very rough sea and no other vessel would take him out to attend to the sick person.

Opposite: A ship's steward is stretchered ashore by the Walmer lifeboat. An emergency appendectomy saved his life with only a few hours to spare.

* This part of the coast, just inside the Goodwin Sands, was a favoured assembly point for wartime convoys.

Walmer sea-front today. An Atlantic
75 ridged-inflatable lifeboat is now
on station there.

Walmer lifeboat station in 1939.

The lifeboat obliged but, in spite of getting the *Mirza*'s position from the convoy's guard-ship and after searching for four hours in the darkness and pouring rain, she was forced to return to Walmer without locating the steamer. They put out again next morning and this time found the right ship and the doctor was able to tend his patient and then return to shore.

Eight hours later, while the weather was still bad and in failing light, the call came again for a doctor to go to another medical emergency, this time aboard a Greek steamer, the *Panachrandos*. To everyone's frustration aboard the lifeboat, the ship was not to be found in the somewhat vague position given for her as 'a mile from the Goodwin Fork Buoy'. Neighbouring ships, including the guide-ship, could not help and the lifeboat returned to station after another fruitless four-hour search, knowing that someone out there was seriously ill with acute appendicitis.

Daylight the next morning finally revealed the elusive *Panachrandos* to the lifeboat coxswain and in tricky conditions he manoeuvred the lifeboat alongside. The doctor was put aboard where he found a very sick ship's steward. The patient was hurriedly manhandled aboard the lifeboat and brought ashore to a waiting ambulance. His emergency appendectomy saved his life with only a few hours to spare.

25 Mersey Pilot Boat Wrecked

26 November 1939

The 434-ton pilot boat, *Charles Livingston*, belonging to the Mersey Docks and Harbour Board, is at sea, cruising on the second pilotage station at the entrance to the River Mersey. She has thirty-three men on board, eleven of them pilots, three trainee pilots and the rest crew. She will be spending a week on her station, providing pilots for every ship about to enter the Mersey.

It is midnight on 25 November 1939 and the weather is filthy and getting worse. The sea is being whipped up by a strong west-south-westerly breeze and heavy rain squalls are sweeping in across the Irish Sea. The second master, Ernest Bibby, curses his luck for getting this watch as he peers through the rain, keeping the Liverpool Bar Lightship in view, about a mile up-weather.

Then, to his exasperation, the lightship's reassuring flashes disappear. Has he been swept further east from his position than he intended? He puts the engines at slow ahead and heads west by south into wind and sea looking all the time for the light. For the next three and a half hours, with ever-increasing concern, he sees nothing, changing course occasionally in the hope of getting back to his original station.

Where is he? It is time to take soundings; three and a half fathoms; now only two and a half. He puts the engines full speed ahead and the helm hard over. The boat will not answer the helm. As she sinks into a trough, her movement is interrupted by a thud and all the fittings on the bridge rattle. It is the bottom. Then she strikes again, much more violently than before, then again, and again.

By now the captain, Alexander McLeod, is on deck, yelling at the crew to let go both anchors, but it is too late, they do not hold and the *Charles Livingston* is driven before the wind further and further into shallow water. Eventually the bumping and shuddering stops as the boat's flat bottom jams against a sandbank and she takes on an alarming list. Powerful seas begin to smash against her side, many of them breaking over the deck. Both master and second master know that high tide is seven hours away (at about ten thirty), and that if she does not refloat, she will soon be awash.

Two things to do: call for help and get the vessel's boats in the water, ready to take the crew off if necessary. Flares, rockets and maroons are fired, the whistle is sounded and a message goes via radio telephone to the Docks and Harbour

Opposite: Rescuers from the shore rush out to meet Blackpool lifeboat, *Sarah Ann Austin*, after her coxswain and crew had taken off the last survivors from the doomed Mersey pilot boat, *Charles Livingston*.

At low tide the sands at Ainsdale and Southport stretch virtually as far as the eye can see.
(*Edward Wake-Walker*)

the sound of explosions, apparently coming from out at sea. Looking through his bedroom window on Ainsdale promenade, he could see red flares and realised that these were signals of distress.

Brown was a lifeguard who, in the summer, worked at the Ainsdale Bathing Centre, situated between towering dunes inland and the vast stretches of tidal sands that are such a feature along the Lancashire coast between Formby and the Ribble estuary.* In the winter, when there was no call for lifeguards, Bob Brown kept himself fit on the rugby field as the wing three-quarter for the Rochdale Hornets.

His first reaction to the signals was to check with the night watchman they had been seen by others. He was assured that Southport police were on their way along with ambulance crews, firemen and many other helpers; there was, however, no local rocket brigade to call upon. Brown then sprinted across the undulating sands, out towards the water's edge. He could see the lights of two masts which were no more than 500yds out to sea. As he half waded, half swam out through the surf, he could make out the outline of a vessel in the intermittent moonlight with a tall, central funnel. He could also see men moving purposefully about on deck. Brown, who had now been joined by others on the beach, later recounted:

Board that they are ashore somewhere on the North Wales coast between the Mersey and Great Orme Head by Llandudno, a stretch of some 30 miles.

The two motor boats and a rowing boat are swung from their davits and lowered gingerly into the water. A young apprentice is aboard the rowing boat and there are two crew members in each of the motor boats as they are all brought along the *Charles Livingston*'s lee side to be secured. Suddenly the rowing boat breaks free and drifts off into the darkness. Both motor boats immediately cast off and give chase. The five men are never to be seen alive again.

Bob Brown thought that the war had finally got going when he was woken in the early hours by

Whether they could see us I do not know, but we gained the impression that the crew had decided to remain on board in an endeavour to refloat their ship on the incoming tide.

The engines were racing madly and the boat was shuddering from stem to stern. We went back to the shore and later guided police officers towards the boat but by that time the water had got deeper and when we were up to our waists, we found it was impossible to go further.

We next tried to launch our own little lifeboat which has a 7hp engine but it would not stand up to the fury of the waves. Twice it overturned with the crew of four in the water and in the end, after six attempts, we had to give it up. We then got a rowing boat out but the oars snapped like matchwood and we had to give that up also.

* The famous Royal Birkdale golf course nestles among these dunes and, a few decades later, the sands would be where the racehorse, Red Rum, was to exercise and build up his renowned stamina.

All we could do was to keep a close watch on the beach, patrolling unceasingly, watching for any of the crew who might be washed ashore.

By this time, people on shore were beginning to ask themselves why there was no sign of a lifeboat. Surely someone had called them out? It should not have taken crews from New Brighton or Lytham St Anne's much more than an hour to get to Ainsdale, even in these atrocious conditions.

The reason may well be obvious to the reader: the vessel ashore at Ainsdale was the *Charles Livingston*. Three motor lifeboats were indeed out looking for her but they were up to 30 miles away, scouring the sandy coastline of North Wales. If ever there was an occasion where ship-to-shore radio would have helped the lifeboat service, this was it. Of the six lifeboats that would eventually be called to help the *Charles Livingston*, only one, New Brighton's No. 1 lifeboat, *William and Kate Johnston*, was fitted with a radio. And for the moment, she was on her mooring at her station.

When the pilot boat originally radioed that she was aground off the coast of Wales, Hoylake, Rhyl and New Brighton No. 2 lifeboats put out to her.* There was no way of recalling them when, finally, at about eight twenty, their honorary secretaries received the message that the vessel they were looking for was on the Lancashire coast. Still exhausted from their exertions the previous day, the New Brighton No. 1 lifeboat crew cast off in search of her.

Twenty miles to the north, Lytham St Anne's lifeboat, *Dunleary*, had already set out, her crew equally shattered. They had been out all night rescuing fifteen men from a stranded trawler and had just returned. The Lytham St Anne's coxswain, John Parkinson, did not know what he

One of the *Charles Livingston*'s motor boats washed ashore at Ainsdale: the occupants were among those who were lost. (*Pathé*)

* The larger New Brighton No. 1 lifeboat and her crew had just returned from a 14-hour service to a passenger liner, *Pegu*, saving 103 lives.

The upper reaches of the Ribble estuary at Lytham.

was searching for. All he knew was that the coastguard had spotted rockets to the south. The landward view from the deck of the lifeboat that morning was one of heavy breaking seas, spume and spray. There was no sign of any vessel.

Both he and the New Brighton lifeboat eventually gave up the search. On his way back to station the New Brighton No. 1 coxswain came upon his No. 2 station boat and the Hoylake lifeboat, both of which had finally abandoned their North Wales search and,

arriving back at their station, had learned the true position of the wreck. Convinced by the New Brighton No. 1 coxswain that there was nothing to be found, all three boats returned home.

Meanwhile, there is only one hope left aboard the *Charles Livingston* now that their boats have disappeared along with the young men aboard them: maybe their vessel will refloat as the tide comes in. But the tide and strengthening gale are in no mood to help them. Walls of brownish water, 20ft high, tower above the vessel before sweeping over her decks, knocking every man off his feet in the pandemonium of their passing.

In the aftermath of one of these huge waves, Captain McLeod realises that any hope of saving his boat has gone. The engine-room skylight has succumbed to the onslaught and water is pouring on to the machinery and into the hull compartments. Worse still, he has just seen a number of his crew swept overboard. Men are now scrambling to get as high up the vessel as they can. There is room in the rigging for some but others are clinging to the wheelhouse roof and other parts of the superstructure.

The six men in the rigging can only watch in despair as the tide rises and wave after wave crashes over the deck below. They see their captain lose his fight for a handhold and disappear. Then the bridge is torn away along with the men who were relying upon it. One by one, with ruthless persistence, the waves winkle the rest of the men on the deck from their refuge. Eventually, only the six in the rigging remain.

As the daylight comes they can see the outline of the shore and to their consternation recognise their true position on Ainsdale Sands. Only 500yds away, across the spray-filled surface of the sea, they can make out a crowd of people on the beach. They allow themselves a glimmer of hope. Even if a lifeboat cannot get to them, the tide will peak at 10.30 and probably recede enough for them to walk ashore; if they have enough strength to stay aloft for another eight hours, that is.

It was a grim morning for the rescuers on the sands. Body after body had come ashore, they counted twenty-two in all.* Only four men were spared by the sea. One of them was the second master, Ernest Bibby, two others were pilots and the fourth was a nineteen-year-old apprentice, Robert Teire. He had been able to rid himself of his sea boots, oilskins and jersey when he found himself in the sea. He had managed to keep himself afloat for two hours in the icy water and eventually reached shore semi-conscious. He was picked up by a horseman who had joined the search for survivors.

The men in the rigging were quite obvious now to the people on the beach. They had climbed as high up the masts as they could as seas clawed at their footholds and covered them with spray. At the tide's height, only 4ft of the funnel was visible. No wonder a lifeboat had not been able to spot anything from the sea.

By mid-morning, however, two lifeboats were once again on their way to Ainsdale. This time they had been given an exact position to aim for and knew for certain that there were men who needed rescuing. One was the Lytham St Anne's lifeboat setting out for a third time within twelve hours; the other was the *Sarah Ann Austin* from Blackpool under the command of Coxswain William Parr.

It was an extremely rough passage for both lifeboats, especially Blackpool's Liverpool class which, at 35ft 6in, was nearly 10ft shorter than the Lytham Watson. The more powerful Watson class reached the scene first, her coxswain moving cautiously towards the two masts and funnel which were all he could see of the wreck. Closer still, he could make out two men in the rigging. Four more emerged for a moment from the cabin.

The decks were still awash but the tide was now ebbing quickly. The lifeboat ran in under the lee of the pilot boat and made fast. Almost immediately her crew felt her strike the bottom and they urged the men to come on board. To their astonishment, the men refused, saying that they would now wait until the tide had ebbed sufficiently for them to walk ashore. The coxswain, concerned that he would soon be stranded himself and convinced by the survivors that they could last out, cut the rope and pulled clear. Seeing that the Blackpool lifeboat had now arrived on scene, he set course for home.

The Blackpool coxswain, knowing he had a much shallower draft, took his lifeboat straight in alongside the wreck. By now it was 2 p.m. and the men of the *Charles Livingston* had been stranded for more than ten hours. They decided that had been long enough and this time accepted the offer of rescue. The lifeboat, expertly handled, made straight for the beach with the

---

* One other man was lost but his body was not immediately found.

exhausted men. Willing hands rushed into the sea to carry them ashore.

On her way home, the Blackpool lifeboat nearly suffered a tragedy of her own. A wave suddenly caught the boat broadside on and two crew members, Frank Cornall and Jack Gerrard, were thrown overboard. Gerrard's hand found the lifeline round the boat but Cornall had surfaced 20yds away. Coxswain Parr swung the boat around and with swift and skilful action by the crew, the two men were hauled to safety from the water.

A Ministry of Shipping inquiry into the wreck of the *Charles Livingston* passed a heavy censure on the second master of the pilot boat and put the lifeboats' late arrival entirely down to wrong information from the casualty about her position. The coxswains of Blackpool and Lytham St Anne's both received the RNLI Silver Medal for gallantry and their respective motor mechanics the Bronze.

Opposite: Coxswain William Parr of Blackpool (standing behind the town's Mayoress and to the right of the Mayor), with his crew and the lifeboat used in the rescue on Ainsdale beach.

26 Enemy Mines Take Their Toll

Margate, 1-2 December 1939

Crowds of people rushed from shops and offices to the seafront and jetty at Margate on the morning of Friday 1 December 1939, drawn by the increasingly familiar sound of an explosion out at sea. The approaches to the Thames estuary had become a prime target for German mine-layers and the people of the north Kent coast had the dubious privilege of a front-row view of the havoc they were causing.

The watchers were greeted by the sight of a cargo vessel sitting lamely in the water and a pall of black smoke hanging over her bow. Next they heard the rumble of the town's lifeboat gathering speed down the slipway on the pier and saw the white plume of water as her bow parted the surface of the sea. Those with binoculars could make out men on the deck of the stricken ship preparing to launch the lifeboats. They had already got one in the water by the time the Margate lifeboat, *The Lord Southborough* (*Civil Service No. 1*),* had drawn alongside.

There were thirty-seven men aboard the 4,500-ton Newcastle steamship *Dalryan*, when she hit the mine. Although the explosion showered the wheelhouse with debris from the cargo hold, the only injury was a broken wrist to a man blown into the air by the blast. Margate's coxswain, Edward Drake Parker,** found a remarkable air of calm emanating from the captain and crew as they efficiently gathered their luggage and clambered aboard the lifeboat.

By the time the lifeboat had pulled away from the cargo ship's side, however, she had begun to go down fast by the head. With cries of 'Look! There she goes!', the thousands on the sea-front saw the bow dip below the waves as her stern slowly rose high into the air before slithering, as if down a steep slope, beneath the surface.

---

* Employees of the UK Civil Service and Post Office have for many years run an annual appeal among themselves to fund lifeboats for the RNLI. To this day, forty-two lifeboats have carried the 'Civil Service' suffix to their name.

** Edward Drake Parker would go on to win the Distinguished Service Medal for the part he played in the Dunkirk evacuation in 1940 as one of only two RNLI coxswains to accompany their lifeboats to the French beaches. He was responsible for bringing off some 600 men.

Opposite: Survivors of the mined oil tanker, *San Calisto*, are landed alongside Margate pier by the lifeboat, *The Lord Southborough* (*Civil Service No. 1*).

One man brought ashore by the lifeboat claimed that it had been his most comfortable shipwreck to date. Able Seaman Henry Bladburn of New Brighton, who had been mined and torpedoed three times in the previous war and twice shipwrecked since, was very appreciative of the fact that this time he had escaped without a wetting.

Twenty-four hours later, just before noon on 2 December, two more massive explosions were heard at Margate in quick succession, this time probably from a little further out to sea. Most of the lifeboat crew were in the boathouse when they heard it, so the lifeboat was in the water with minimum delay. About 2 miles east by north of the Tongue Light-vessel she came across a number of minesweepers clustered around an oil-tanker which was quite clearly sinking. She was the 8,000-ton *San Calisto* of London and another victim of a mine.

One of the minesweepers, *Stella Leonis*, flashed a signal to the lifeboat, asking her to come alongside. She had twelve survivors from the tanker aboard and wanted Coxswain Drake Parker to get them ashore. The coxswain took them aboard and then headed for the tanker herself. He wanted to be sure that no one had been left behind. Two of his crew went on board the sinking ship and carried out a rapid but thorough search. They found nothing and rejoined the lifeboat.

The crew of the Newcastle steamship, *Dalryan*, come ashore after 'the most comfortable shipwreck to date'. (*Pathé*)

During the Second World War, calls were so frequent that Margate lifeboat crew often kept watch at the lifeboat station. Here, a game of cribbage is in progress.

Margate lifeboat launches from her station on the pier during the war.

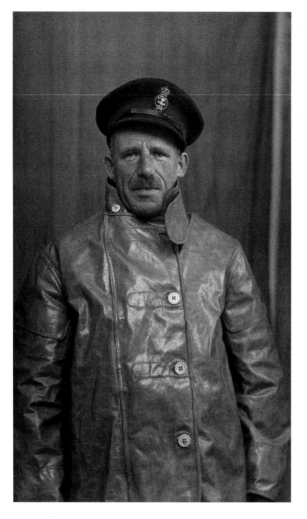

Margate's famous wartime coxswain, Edward Drake Parker. He was responsible for evacuating some six hundred troops from the beaches of Dunkirk.

Opposite: The BBC making a broadcast from Margate lifeboat station on 17 October 1942. Ted Parker, the coxswain, is being interviewed by F. More O'Ferrall. The coxswain's brother, Harry, is in the foreground and his son, Ted jnr, nearest to the lifeboat, is talking to the BBC's Raymond Glendenning, decked out in oilskins and with sou'wester in hand.

couldn't be transferred without medical attention.

The coxswain therefore made for the jetty at Margate where he discharged his human cargo, embarked ambulance men and returned to the minesweeper. The injured man received first aid and was then taken ashore by the lifeboat. Another fifteen men were brought ashore by two Margate motor boats that had also been summoned to land survivors from vessels on the scene.

This had been no 'comfortable shipwreck' for the survivors. One of the youngest, Able Seaman Gilbert Hay was in the crow's nest when the first explosion blew the ship apart under the bridge. The second blast broke the vessel's back. He later recalled: 'Most of the boats were smashed. Only two boatloads got away and the rest of the men were stranded on the poop.' He was also continually asking his shipmates and rescuers: 'Have you seen my pal?' When a roll-call was eventually taken, it transpired that his pal was one of five men missing, presumed drowned.

The man whose body the lifeboat landed had been on his last voyage before retiring at the age of sixty-one. He was Ernest Whearley, the ship's carpenter and a veteran of the First World War, during which he had been badly injured by a mine.

The ship's captain, Albert Hicks of St Ives, had a lucky escape. He was the last to leave the ship and had to jump into the sea with an injured hand and knee. He clung on to the wreckage of one of the ship's boats until he was picked up.

As the mines struck, the cook, Charles Belcher of the Queen's Arms, Gravesend, could only remember his huge disappointment that the special lunch he had just prepared of turtle soup, roast mutton, cabbage, baked and boiled potatoes and ginger pudding would now only go to feed the fishes.

Another minesweeper, the *Hugh Walpole*, hailed the lifeboat as she headed for home. They had the body of a *San Calisto* crewman on board which they wanted to transfer. Then, a little nearer Margate, the lifeboat encountered another minesweeper with eleven survivors of the blast on board. Ten of them were put aboard the lifeboat but one was in a bad way and

27 Aground at Thurlestone

Belgian Cargo Vessel, *Louis Sheid*, 7 December 1939

*K*orvettenkapitän Günther Prien might well have felt a wave of satisfaction at another job well done as his torpedo hit home with resounding effect against the hull of the cargo vessel steaming eastward through the Channel.

It would be difficult ever to equal the prize he had claimed less than two months earlier when he had taken his submarine, *U-47*, into the sheltered Orkney waters of Scapa Flow and sunk the British battleship, HMS *Royal Oak*, along with 833 of her crew. Hitler himself had presented him with the Knight's Cross with Oak Leaves for that adventure. But this early morning's work could only help to demoralise the enemy's merchant navy war effort.

The vessel the lieutenant-commander had hit, at five thirty in the morning of Thursday 7 December 1939, was the 8,000-ton Dutch freighter *Tajandoen*, which had left Amsterdam the day before bound for Batavia in the Dutch East Indies. She was carrying a general cargo as well as fourteen passengers including five women and two children.

It took only 15 minutes for the ship to sink but in that time, miraculously, all the passengers and crew, except two engineers and four seamen, believed killed in the explosion, made it into a lifeboat. The torpedo had split open the ship's fuel tanks and the sea was ablaze with burning oil. The men at the oars of the four lifeboats had to pull for their lives away from the sinking ship as the flames raced across the sea towards them.

Thankfully for the sixty-two survivors, two other ships had heard the explosion and were now approaching the scene. One was the Italian steamer *Georgio Ohlsen* and the other a Belgian vessel, the *Louis Sheid*, returning from Buenos Aires with a cargo of grain, animal hides, leaf tobacco and honey. The two captains agreed that it would make more sense for the *Louis Sheid* to take on the survivors as she was bound for Antwerp, reasonably close to their home.

The 6,000-ton *Louis Sheid* was originally a German ship, the *Ultor*, then becafme the *Kendal Castle* under Liverpool ownership and acquired her ultimate name when sold to the Belgian National Shipping Line. In this time of war it was not her name, however, which was important to recognise but her nationality. 'BELGIE' was painted in large white letters on her side to let

Opposite: The crew of the *Louis Sheid* are hauled ashore by breeches buoy in Bigbury Bay after the Belgian steamer ran aground evading U-boats.

141

Salcombe's brand new, twin-screw Watson class lifeboat, *Samuel and Marie Parkhouse*.

any prowling periscope know that she came from a neutral country.

The captain soon realised, though, as the *Tajandoen*'s survivors came aboard his ship, that neutrality did not seem to count for much in the eyes of German U-boats. Holland was also a neutral country but that had not saved the Dutch ship. Mindful of the safety of the 107 people now on board his ship, he decided that he should steer towards the south Devon coast and shallower water where a U-boat might be loath to follow.

The weather was getting worse and by nightfall a full southerly gale was blowing and the outline of land had disappeared in heavy squalls of rain.

At about seven in the evening the villagers of Thurlestone were blinking in disbelief through their rain-spattered windows at the sight of a brightly lit ship, apparently under power, heading straight for their rocky shore. She made an incongruous spectacle in the pitch darkness of a wartime blackout as she sailed blindly on until there came the inevitable sound of metal hull grinding against granite reef.

The *Louis Sheid* had become a victim of her own defence mechanism. She had come too far inshore on her north-eastern bearing and, without the help of any lights on shore and in very poor visibility, had run aground in Bigbury Bay.

A mile and a half further south at Hope Cove, Jack Jarvis, coxswain of the lifeboat before the station closed, had also witnessed the grounding. His first reaction was to telephone Salcombe lifeboat station. He knew that with a southerly gale and the tide at four hours ebb, conditions on the bar at Salcombe could not be much worse, and he wouldn't blame Eddie Distin, the Salcombe coxswain, for waiting.

But within ten minutes of his call, the station's brand new, twin-screw Watson class lifeboat, *Samuel and Marie Parkhouse*, was heading out of the harbour. The bar at Salcombe had such a reputation that this lifeboat carried special modifications to help her coxswain cope with its lethal tendencies. She had a shallower draft than the normal Watson, her turtle-decks fore and aft shed water more quickly and her stern frame was strengthened to protect rudder and propellers should she touch the bottom. A sterner test could not have been devised for these capabilities as the lifeboat headed out that night on her very first rescue mission.

The station honorary secretary had taken the precaution of asking a local boat to stand by inside the harbour in case of an accident. Her skipper was soon able to report, however, that the coxswain's handling had been masterful as the lifeboat corkscrewed, climbed and plummeted through the near vertical breaking seas which reared up angrily over the shallow bar.

That danger passed, the lifeboat rounded Bolt Head to be met broadside on by mountains of water rolling in across the Channel on the southerly gale. It was two hours before the coxswain drew close to the *Louis Sheid*. He found her almost head on to wind and sea, about half a mile from the shore; her engines were going full speed ahead, but the ship was going nowhere.

The coxswain first tried veering down on his anchor to get along the starboard side but there were too many rocks close by. He then lifted his anchor and made for the port side. Although there was a small amount of lee, the lifeboat was still falling and rising some 20 to 30ft against the side of the freighter. The captain was anxious to get the people he had rescued from the *Tajandoen* ashore as soon as possible, so, one by one and with crucial timing, forty of them were thrust into the lifeboatmen's outstretched arms as the lifeboat surged up towards the level of the ship's deck.

Meanwhile, at Hope Cove, Jack Jarvis had been preparing to receive the Dutch survivors. His three sons and other men had a 16ft pulling boat ready so that when the lifeboat arrived at a point just inside Bolt Tail, her decks crowded, she was met by the boat and the people were taken ashore through powerful surf, eight at a time.

By the time the lifeboat arrived back at the grounded ship, she had shifted a little and was dead head on to the seas so there was no lee offered. The starboard side was clearer of the rocks, however, so the coxswain chose this side to approach this time. In an equally nerve-racking operation, the remaining twenty-two from the Dutch ship were got aboard the lifeboat and taken to Hope Cove where the local men rowed them ashore.

On the lifeboat's return to the *Louis Sheid*, it was clear to the coxswain that her entire ship's company of forty-five intended to stay put, at least for the time being. The ship had moved again and was now much closer and broadside on to the shore, right over the reef on which she had stranded. He saw that the coastguard's lifesaving apparatus team had fired a line across to her, so there was a means of getting the crew off from the land. He also saw that the Plymouth lifeboat, *Robert and Marcella Beck*, had made it to the scene.

Both lifeboats stood by throughout the night until, in daylight, the crew were eventually hauled ashore by breeches buoy. Only then did both boats return to their stations.

Edwin Distin deservedly won the RNLI Silver Medal for this rescue and each of his crew the Bronze for their remarkable efforts in getting sixty-two people off the ship without injury. The *Louis Sheid* never got off the reef. Some of her cargo was salvaged and some metal from her hull was cut up and reused for the war effort. Parts of her structure can still be seen from the shore at low water.

28 Bomb Attack off the Norfolk Coast

9 February 1940

With the wartime threat of hidden enemy mines and torpedoes adding to the normal hazards of navigating close to the British Isles in winter, the sound of an aircraft engine came as another perpetual source of anxiety to merchant skippers.

It was just before noon on 9 February 1940 when the *Boston Trader*, a 371-ton coasting steamer of Great Yarmouth, was passing Cley next the Sea on the north Norfolk coast. A stiff, icy wind was blowing from the east and the small ship was being buffeted in rough seas. One of her crew became aware of a deep humming, increasingly audible above the wind and the familiar sound of his vessel's own engine. He looked skywards and to the east. Other eyes on deck followed his.

At first they saw nothing, then the dark shape of an aircraft materialised out of the grey cloud, flying lower all the time and passing almost directly overhead. It flew on westward and the coaster's crewmen held their breath. They had all seen the marking under the wing; it was an enemy plane. Then they saw what they had been dreading: the plane was banking steeply ahead of them and coming straight back at the coaster.

As they dived for cover, the plane's engines grew to a roar, accompanied by staccato bursts of machine-gun fire. There was an explosion on board as the plane unleashed a dozen bombs and then flew off towards the Norfolk coast.

The *Boston Trader*'s crew would not have seen, a few moments later, the same aircraft being chased out to sea by three British planes. They were too busy launching their lifeboat amid the smoke and flames which had taken hold of their ship. Two had been injured by machine-gun fire but all seven men were alive and able to get aboard the lifeboat.

News reached Sheringham lifeboat station almost immediately that they were needed and the single-engined Liverpool class lifeboat, *Foresters' Centenary*, put out at twelve thirty-three. Homing in on the plume of smoke, it did not take her long to come across the seven men in the ship's lifeboat. The coxswain took them on board, then steered towards the abandoned steamer to see if she could be saved. However, it was soon clear that she was so badly damaged and so thoroughly on fire that nothing could be done. The photographs shows the survivors returning to dry land on Sheringham beach, a final piggy-back being all part of the lifeboat service.

Opposite and overleaf, top: The crew of the SS *Boston Trader* are carried ashore by Sheringham lifeboatmen after their ship was destroyed by a German aircraft.

A wartime lifeboat crew observing
aircraft activity.

Sheringham lifeboat house sits hard up against the cliff, parallel to the shore.

29 Dunkirk Battle Wounds

Clacton's lifeboat repaired, 25 July 1940

The phenomenon of the Victorian seaside pier, built to provide ozone-rich amusement and embarkation points for tourist trips round the bay, has for many years had the added benefit of helping the RNLI at several locations round the coast. To this day, lifeboats at such places as The Mumbles, Weston-super-Mare, Cromer, Southend and Clacton are launched from the end of the town's pier, ensuring that they can get away at all states of the tide.

The boathouse and slipway extending from the pier at Clacton in Essex meant, with the advent of motor lifeboats, that the RNLI was not confined to using small lifeboats, light enough to be pulled on a carriage to the water's edge. The *Edward Z. Dresden*, delivered to the station in 1929, was a powerful 45ft 6in Watson class with twin 40hp engines, a speed of more than 8 knots and excellent sea-keeping capabilities.

In the 1930s she was kept busy in an area very popular with yachtsmen and where sailing barges plied a brisk trade. Her coxswain, Charlie Ellis, was recognised by the RNLI with its official thanks inscribed on vellum for rescuing a German yacht and her crew in a violent sea in June 1938.

Then he received the Silver Medal in November 1939 for putting out twice in a gale, first to rescue three men from a swamped fishing smack and then for plucking two men from the rigging of a barge, having driven his lifeboat Henry Blogg-style (see Chapter 13) over the deck.

When Coxswain Ellis and his crew set out from Clacton late on 30 May 1940, following the request by RNLI headquarters to report to Dover, along with eighteen other lifeboats, for 'special duty' under the Admiralty, it was difficult to know what they had let themselves in for. They had done their best to prepare, taking extra rations and medical supplies, guessing it had something to do with evacuating troops. Whatever it was, they were ready to play their part.

Arriving at the entrance to Dover harbour with seven other RNLI lifeboats on the morning of 31 May, they were met by a naval launch, given a course for Dunkirk and sent into the harbour to refuel. To their bafflement and indignation, no sooner were they inside the harbour than naval staff ordered them out of their boats and took them over.

What they did not know was that there had been an argument between the coxswains of the

Opposite: Clacton lifeboat, *Edward Z. Dresden*, undergoing repairs on the River Colne after returning from the beaches of Dunkirk.

Hythe, Walmer and Dungeness lifeboats and Navy officers the previous evening when they had arrived with their boats at Dover. The Hythe coxswain, Henry Griggs, had tried to persuade the Navy that his instructions to run his lifeboat on to the beach at Dunkirk, load her with troops and bring them out to ships, would fail. His 14-ton boat would never come off the beach. The Walmer and Dungeness lifeboats were even heavier.

Failing to win his argument, he then asked to be shown in writing what pension his crew's families might expect, should they fail to return, something he fully expected. This, the Navy could or would not do and so the three coxswains and their crews said they could not go to Dunkirk. The Navy took their boats and gave the crews railway vouchers for their journey home.

The result of this impasse (for which the RNLI later felt compelled to dismiss the Hythe coxswain and his mechanic)* was to persuade the Navy that it could not waste any more precious time in negotiation with lifeboat crews and that it would use its own men in all the other boats provided by the RNLI. The exceptions were the Margate and Ramsgate lifeboat crews who had already gone to Dunkirk the night before. Between them, under frequent bombardment, these two boats brought 3,400 to safety off the beaches.

No detailed record exists of the exploits of the remaining seventeen commandeered lifeboats. They all played an important part in the evacuation and all eventually returned with the exception of the Hythe lifeboat. This boat had been seen by the Ramsgate coxswain approaching the beach.

The *Edward Z. Dresden* ready for service on her slipway on Clacton pier.

* Coxswain Griggs had held his position at Hythe for twenty years and had won the RNLI's thanks on vellum and the Silver Medal for gallantry. Two months after his dismissal he launched his own fishing boat to rescue two British airmen from a crashed bomber.

The coast at Clacton with the lifeboat slipway just visible jutting out on the left-hand side of the pier.

She was put aground; soldiers waded out to her and she stuck fast, just as her coxswain had predicted. She never moved again and was ultimately abandoned, too badly damaged to recover.

The Eastbourne lifeboat had eventually to be abandoned by the naval officer in charge of her but only after she had been rammed by a torpedo boat and twice sprayed with 500 rounds of machine-gun bullets. Two days later she was found drifting in the English Channel, her fore-end box stove in and peppered with bullet holes. She was full of water but still upright and afloat. She was towed back to Dover, and after extensive repairs, returned to her station in April 1941.

The *Edward Z. Dresden* of Clacton was taken inside the harbour at Dunkirk and, until daybreak on 4 June, was used to ferry troops to ships standing by outside the entrance. On her way home across the Channel, she was attacked by a German fighter plane. The damage was not severe but it did require a visit to the boatyard at Rowhedge, up the River Colne, to patch up the bullet holes. The picture on page 148 shows the work in progress.

When, in August, she was again ready for service, she could not immediately return to her station. The Ministry of Home Defence had ordered that all piers should be disabled to deny a landing stage to invading forces and a yawning gap now separated Clacton lifeboat station from the landward end of the pier. Some of the lifeboat crew and their families took up temporary residence in nearby Brightlingsea where the lifeboat was stationed on a mooring until a bridging arrangement could be negotiated with the MoHD.

30 Steamer Disabled

Sheringham, 30 October 1941

In his book, *Storm on the Waters*, an excellent record of the lifeboat service during the Second World War, written in 1946, the RNLI's publicity secretary Charles Vince recounts the following story:

One morning at Sheringham, after a night of gale, the landlord of an inn on the sea-front was serving in his bar. There was a fog on the sea but the sun suddenly shone through. As it did so the landlord looked up and in that sudden increase of light saw a speck about two miles out at sea. He put his telescope on to it. The sea was rough and the speck kept disappearing, but it seemed to him like men on a raft.

Just then the second coxswain of the lifeboat came in for a glass of beer. He went off at once with the news and the lifeboat was launched. She found that speck to be a rubber dinghy with five Polish airmen on board. Their bomber had crashed in the gale of the night before and for 17 hours they had drifted and tossed unseen in the fog, without food, soaked, seasick, until that sudden gleam of the sun and the quick eye of the landlord had brought them the lifeboat.

It was only two days after that heartening event when, as another very strong gale from the north-east was making its presence felt on the town, news came through that there was another likely job for the lifeboat. There was a ship off Cley next the Sea, 5 miles along the coast to the west, which had signalled to the Coastguard that she was out of control.

Conditions were so bad that the honorary secretary did not want to send the lifeboat out unless or until he knew she was definitely required. No distress signal had yet been given, so the lifeboat crew waited in the boathouse. Five hours passed and, at one on the morning of 30 October, a message came that the ship had drifted to within a mile of Cley and that she was calling for a tug. The coastguard had signalled that a tug was out of the question in that weather but that the lifeboat was standing by to launch. The skipper signalled back that he would let them know if and when he needed a lifeboat.

Another eight hours passed and the weather had moderated, but only by a little. The wind was still blowing hard straight off a very rough sea and there were hefty squalls of rain and sleet. At nine twenty-three the vessel signalled that she was drifting and needed help.

In wartime there was a scarcity of lifeboat launchers whose job it was to heave the 7-ton motor lifeboat on her carriage from the boathouse

Opposite: Members of the *Eaglescliffe Hall's* Canadian crew celebrate their return to dry land in a very British way.

153

to the water's edge. On this occasion the tide was low so the handful of men had a real struggle manhandling their load down the steep, pebble beach through a narrow, sea-filled channel and over a sandbank. The wheels of the carriage stuck in the sandbank and it took much straining to get clear.

Eventually the carriage was in deep water and the *Foresters' Centenary* got away. The sea was comparatively calm at the launching point because it had been broken by an outlying ledge of rocks, exposed at low tide. Now Coxswain James Dumble would have to steer the lifeboat through a narrow channel in this ledge to make it to the open sea. Heavy seas were breaking over the ledge and the launchers looked on anxiously as the lifeboat disappeared, then reappeared in clouds of spray and white water as she forced her way through the gap.

On deck, the crew visibly relaxed as they found themselves clear and in deep water, heading along the coast towards Cley. They soon found the ship in trouble; she was a 1,900-ton Canadian steamer, the *Eaglescliffe Hall*. She was still afloat in about four fathoms of water, head to sea with two anchors down. She had a lot of wires and buoys trailing from her propeller, having obviously drifted through a boom defence.

The lifeboat made fast alongside and the captain agreed that fifteen of his men should be taken ashore while he and eight others remained aboard as the weather was now easing. The fifteen Canadians were taken back to Sheringham where they were given every hospitality. By the following day the weather had further improved and the lifeboat took the men back to their ship where a tug had come to tow her to eventual safety.

Opposite: A Sheringham pub landlord re-enacts the moment when he and the lifeboat second coxswain spotted five Polish airmen adrift on a liferaft, 2 miles out to sea.

Coxswain James Dumble. He received the Bronze bravery medal for his exceptional boat handling in getting the lifeboat clear of the surf to rescue the crew of the *Eaglescliffe Hall*.

Coxswain Dumble's skilful and courageous boat handling was recognised by the RNLI's Bronze Medal. The *Eaglescliffe Hall* did not survive the war, unfortunately; barely ten months later she was bombed and sunk by an enemy aircraft 2 miles off Sunderland.

31 Launch at Port Erin

17 October 1942

The deep reverberation of the idling engines fill the boathouse, retaining chains clatter to the floor, the crew duck low to avoid the roof beams, the coxswain shouts that he is ready, a metal hammer strikes a metal pin, the lifeboat, free of her last restraint, escapes through the open door, accelerating with every yard. The rumble of her hurtling progress ends abruptly with the swish of startled water leaping from the gash in the sea cut by her bow. For a second the lifeboat seems reluctant to leave the snow-white nest she has created, her stern beds down into the forgiving ocean, but then the propellers bite and she is away.

For anyone witnessing a slipway launch for the first time, it is a thrilling moment and an image they will carry with them for the rest of their lives. There could be no more dramatic entrance on to the rescue scene, no firmer statement of intent. For a lifeboat crew it marks the point of no return; the moment when they have severed their last link with the shore and are out on their mission on their own.

The launch captured by this photograph, taken in October 1942 at Port Erin on the south-west tip of the Isle of Man, was not in answer to any distress, but to honour the retirement of the station's coxswain, Alfred Cregeen, who had been a crew member for forty-five years. Joining up just before the turn of the century, he lived through a period of considerable change as a lifeboatman. In his early days he would have taken an oar in the town's pulling and sailing lifeboat, *William Sugden*, launched from a carriage into the harbour.

Later, in 1925, the slipway in this photograph was built, allowing the station's first motor lifeboat, *Ethel Day Cardwell*, to make the swiftest of getaways at all states of the tide. Then, for the last two years of his tenure, Coxswain Cregeen was the proud operator of the twin-engine Watson class *Matthew Simpson*, shown here hitting the water at low tide with Bradda Head beyond. The lifeboat was to spend thirty-three years at Port Erin, eventually entering the RNLI relief fleet in 1973.

The local paper records that, following this launch, Alfred Cregeen received an RNLI certificate of appreciation and 'a small sum as pension'. Local officials gave him an enlarged portrait of himself and one of the present lifeboat. Cregeen would have been one of the many lifeboatmen who came to the end of a long, dedicated career with no medal to their name and, unlike others remembered in this book, without much media attention.

It was often Douglas, the island's ferry port, and home of the RNLI's founder, Sir William Hillary, which enjoyed more of the limelight. Even so, during Cregeen's time at the station, the lifeboat was called out forty times and twenty lives were saved. More important, he and his fellow crewmen were always ready to go and any seafarer in distress would always have been able to rely on them in his hour of need.

Opposite: In October 1942 the lifeboat was launched down one of the RNLI's longest slipways at Port Erin on the Isle of Man to mark the retirement of her coxswain.

Opposite: Coxswain Alfred Cregeen (front row, centre) with his crew.

Left: Coxswain Alfred Cregeen of Port Erin. He had crewed the lifeboat for forty-five years.

Below: An aerial view of Port Erin with the lifeboat slipway to the left of the harbour wall.

32 Devastation at Sker Point

South Wales, 23 April 1947

It is an utterly desolate scene; the grey light of a reluctant dawn glints off the water of shallow pools and narrow gullies which pockmark the abrasive surface of the low, broad tongue of rock which is Sker Point. Out towards its tip, where it laps at a foaming white sea, two alien shapes disfigure its flatness. One looms massive, dark and angular, the other, a few hundred yards to the east, is a much smaller, rounded, white-capped object. The air is thick with an overpowering stench of oil.

Dimly perceptible are a handful of black-clad figures, arms hung out for balance, picking their way cautiously across the rock towards these shapes. The remnant of last night's storm is still powerful enough occasionally to catch one of them unawares and force him on to hands and knees, before he can regain his feet on the slippery surface. Every so often, one or two of the men stop and crouch, examining what appears to be a clump of seaweed. They turn towards the land and wave urgently to others just emerging through the sand dunes. Then they resume their precarious progress.

'Not this time, Charlie, I don't think!'

True to form, Charlie Davies had turned up at the lifeboat station, ready as ever to make up the crew when he heard the maroon. He had been aboard The Mumbles pulling and sailing lifeboat when she capsized on Port Talbot bar forty-four years previously and survived when six had drowned. He had been one of William Gammon's crew on the night three years ago when the coxswain had won the RNLI Gold Medal after rescuing forty-two Canadian sailors from the torpedoed frigate, *Chebogue*, in a Force 9 gale.

He had been well into his seventies even then, but that was when the station had been short of younger men who were away fighting the war. On this wild April evening in 1947, William Gammon knew he could not afford sentimental favours in choosing his crew. This time the oldest man in the crew would be Ernest Griffin, the assistant mechanic, aged fifty-one.

The radio message from the *Samtampa*, a 7,000-ton British steamship bound from Middlesbrough to Newport in ballast, had been unequivocal and urgent: 'Rapidly drifting towards Nash Shoal'. There was a south-westerly gale blowing and the tide was at half flood. The Mumbles lifeboat was sheltered from the brunt of the weather, but the coxswain was expecting a very rough ride beyond the shelter of Mumbles Head and across Swansea Bay. The lifeboat, *Edward, Prince of Wales*, named

Opposite: Coxswain William Gammon.

after the former President of the RNLI, a single-engine Watson class and veteran of the Gold Medal service, left her slipway at 6.10 p.m.

She had a good 20 miles of ferocious seas to cover to Nash Point, but only 20 minutes into her passage, someone spotted a signal being flashed by The Mumbles coastguard. No one could read it; there was no signalman on board. A fair few lifeboats were carrying radio by 1947, but *Edward, Prince of Wales* was not one of them, being an open boat, without a cabin to protect the equipment.

William Gammon could not ignore the signal, whatever it meant, and turned the lifeboat round to head back to the station. There, from the foot of the slipway, the honorary secretary shouted to the coxswain that the casualty had mistaken her position; she was, in fact, 2½ miles west-north-west from Porthcawl Light, very close to Sker Point. By now it was 7.10 p.m. and the lifeboat set off again immediately, her crew thankful, at least, that it was only half the distance to travel to this new position.

From the shore helpers watched her bucking and burrowing her way across Swansea Bay until her lights finally disappeared from view in the gathering darkness. No one would see the eight men aboard alive again.

The *Samtampa* had been suffering machinery problems as she entered the Bristol Channel on the last leg of her journey before a strong westerly gale. She put down both her anchors in Swansea Bay in the late afternoon. The weather was all the time worsening and, with the wind reaching hurricane force, she put out the message that she was drifting. At 6.20 p.m. she put out another message: 'Have both hooks down and hope to keep off shoal, but doubtful.'

By this time she had been seen by people on the shore and her true position had been relayed to The Mumbles coastguard. Mr G. Price, who was in the clubhouse of the Royal Porthcawl Golf Club and who witnessed as much as any, gave this account:

> Looking out across the channel, I saw a steamer struggling against the storm. As I watched, I could see she appeared out of control and I thought the

Opposite: Seven proud women: six wives and a sister of The Mumbles lifeboatmen who perished in their gallant attempt to save the *Samtampa*'s crew off Sker Point in April 1947. They are seen here on the day they came to London in October of the same year to receive special certificates recording 'the men's devotion to duty and the supreme sacrifice which they had made', at the RNLI's AGM at Central Hall, Westminster. The widows, with their husband's position in parentheses, are, from left to right, Ella Gammon (the coxswain); Elsie Noel (second coxswain); Irene Davies (mechanic); Eileen Thomas (bowman); May Griffin (assistant mechanic); Dinah Howell (crew member) and Dorothy Smith, sister of crew member Richard Smith. Jenny Thomas, wife of the eighth crewmember, William Thomas, was unfortunately unwell and could not attend the ceremony.

The barren rockscape at Sker Point. (*Edward Wake-Walker*)

A high tide launch of the *Edward, Prince of Wales*. Only three years before she was lost, she earned her coxswain, William Gammon, the Gold Medal for gallantry for carrying forty-two Canadian sailors to safety from the frigate *Chebogue*.

The Mumbles lifeboat station.

engines must have broken down. Then the steamer began to drift towards the shore and I saw a distress signal. Very soon the coastguards were on the scene.

At 7.30 p.m. the steamer ran on the rocks and 15 minutes later she broke in half. I saw the stern part drift away. Smoke poured out from the side and enveloped the steamer which had a list of 45 degrees. In less than an hour all on board must have been lost. I scanned the channel for the coming of The Mumbles lifeboat, which I had been told had been summoned, but I did not see it.

While the ship was breaking up, coastguards attempted to fire a rocket line aboard the *Samtampa*. Three times they tried and three times the hurricane force wind defeated them. The rockets seemed to stand still in the air before being hurled back again. Even had they been able to rig a breeches buoy, no crewman would probably have survived being hauled across the rocks in that weather. Normally, you can reach the edge of the plateau of rock at Sker Point, even at high tide.

Segments of the *Samtampa* lie high and dry on Sker Point after her entire crew was lost. (*Pathé*)

That night, the winds conspired with a very high spring tide to cover the rocks with breaking seas.

Eventually, at about 2 a.m. on the 24th, when the tide had receded, a single police officer made it across the rocks and clambered on to the after section of the steamer jammed hard against the seaward edge of the plateau. There was not a soul on board and he and other rescuers could only assume that the entire ship's company of thirty-nine men had been lost.

Now they could only wait for daylight. Nothing had been heard from the lifeboat and no one had seen her. Anxiety grew by the hour until, at about 6 a.m., daylight revealed the disfigured outlines of the bow and middle sections of the *Samtampa* lolling, absurdly marooned, on the flat, oil-blackened surface of the rock. Not very far to the east lay the upturned hull of the lifeboat.

All eight bodies of The Mumbles crew were found that day. Most of them were smothered in fuel oil and three of them had cuts about the head, probably caused by the rocks. All wore lifejackets. Three were on the rocks close to the lifeboat; the other five had been carried up the coast to a sandy beach beyond Sker Point.

The rudder, propeller and underside of the lifeboat were unscathed, there was not even a scratch on the paint. Clearly, she had been thrown on to the rock, already upside down and then shoved across its surface by the sea, leaving a trail of splintered mahogany and fittings torn from her deck. The engine was found in good order with the controls correctly set with the throttle at a little over half speed. The inquest revealed that all the lifeboatmen had died from asphyxia by drowning, exacerbated by swallowing fuel oil. The exact cause of the accident would never be certain but most people believed that the lifeboat capsized while working somewhere close to the wreck.

The men who died alongside their 46-year-old coxswain, William Gammon were: William Noel, second coxswain, 42; William Davies, mechanic, 42; Ernest Griffin, assistant mechanic, 51; William Thomas, bowman, 48; William Howell, 32; William Ronald Thomas, 34; and Richard Smith, 35.

All left widows except Richard Smith who had been due to marry three days after the disaster. His uncle, Bob Smith, had been one of the men

lost in the disaster of 1903. A fund was set up by the Mayor of Swansea to supplement the pensions of the eight men's families. Contributions, which came from all over the country, exceeded £90,000.

Remarkably, only eight weeks after the disaster, an entirely new crew, all men of The Mumbles, were enrolled, a relief lifeboat was provided and the station was operational again.

In October that same year, William Gammon's widow, five of the other crew member's wives (the sixth was unwell on the day), and Richard Smith's sister went to the RNLI Annual Meeting in Central Hall, Westminster to receive a special certificate of honour, recording 'the men's devotion to duty and the supreme sacrifice which they had made'.

Opposite, bottom and above: Two memorials to the *Samtampa* disaster: above, a stained-glass window in the parish church of All Saints, Oystermouth, Swansea, and, left, a plaque on the rocks of Sker Point.

33 Lighthouse Keepers Stranded

Wolf Rock, February 1948

Some say that the Wolf Rock, lying 8 miles to the west of Land's End, got its name from the Cornish word '*gwelva*' meaning 'something to look out for'. Others think it evolved from the word 'engulf' and will show you sixteenth-century maps which mark the rock with the word 'gulph'. The most colourful explanation is that the reef used to make a growling sound as waves washed into a hollow rock, and expelled compressed air with audible force.

The story goes that this lupine warning helped sailors to steer clear of the Cornish coast until wreckers, deprived of potential victims, filled the hollow with stones from the mainland and silenced the natural foghorn irreparably. A wolf made out of copper was then cast by counter-wreckers, its wide-open jaws designed to roar when the wind blew into it. The sculpture never made it out to the rock, however, where the sea would soon have destroyed it in any case. Many later attempts by Trinity House to fix day marks to the hazard were swept away by the waves which constantly washed over the rock.

It was therefore an extraordinary feat of dogged engineering when eventually, in 1870, the 135ft Wolf Rock Lighthouse was completed. It had taken eight years to build, during which time an average of only one hour a day could be spent working on the construction. From that day to this, the light, with a 23-mile range, has flashed unerringly every 15 seconds.

Until automation in July 1988, the lighthouse had to be constantly manned to ensure the continuity of the light. How long a tour of duty might last for keepers of the Wolf Rock light would always be in the lap of the weather gods. Their relief depended entirely on whether it was calm enough for a Trinity House launch to get near to the rock and whether they could walk on its slippery surface without being swept away by Atlantic rollers.

In the early weeks of 1948 an unrelenting series of gales kept three Wolf Rock keepers prisoners in their tower for more than a month beyond their intended day of relief. Stanley McClary, the twenty-year-old principal keeper, and his two assistants, John Mudge and Clifford Wheeler, when they eventually made it ashore at Penzance Quay on Saturday 14 February, were astonished to find a great crowd to meet them and several representatives of the national press.

The nation's concern had been growing steadily over the weeks at the thought of three young men alone on an Atlantic rock, pounded by merciless seas, their supplies and fortitude dwindling by the day; public anxiety was

Opposite: A rocket with line attached is fired by the marooned lighthouse keepers on Wolf Rock towards a launch from the Trinity House vessel *Triton*. In this way, the crew were able to pass letters they had written to friends and family on the mainland.

Opposite, top: Launch of the Penlee lifeboat, *W and S.*
(Courtesy of Graham Farr)

Opposite, bottom: The Penlee lifeboat, *Mabel Alice*, in a modern winching exercise with a Sea King helicopter from RNAS Culdrose.

Left: The first time a helicopter had been used to bring relief to lighthouse keepers.
(*Fleet Air Arm Museum, Yeovilton*)

171

becoming almost too difficult to bear. The situation was aggravated by the fact that the lighthouse's radio transmitter had lost its power, so their link with the land had been severed.

Tenuous contact was occasionally possible, as the main photograph shows, when a rocket with line attached was fired by the keepers to the launch from the Trinity House vessel, *Triton*. In this way letters could be passed to and from the mainland in a comparative lull in the winter's onslaught. But as the weather worsened again and few vessels put to sea, it was left to the Newlyn to Isles of Scilly ferry, the *Scillonian*, to get close enough to establish radio communication. A very weak signal was picked up by the ferry which appeared to say that the three keepers had only four days' supply of bully beef left and no other provisions.

In fact, what Stanley McClary had tried to convey was that their emergency supplies of beef, biscuits and tinned flour would last another twenty-seven days, if necessary. He was therefore quite taken aback, four days after his visit from the *Scillonian*, to see the Penlee lifeboat, *W and S*, clawing her way towards them through the seas and utterly dumbfounded to hear the staccato beat of a helicopter overhead. Few people had seen such an aircraft before and now here was one, hovering over the lighthouse, preparing to lower life-preserving rations on to the gallery at the top of the tower. McClary later recalled that the first articles they found as they opened the packages were cigarettes. Apparently, all three men jumped for joy on the gallery.

In a matter of minutes, the helicopter was on its way back to Culdrose and Penlee lifeboat's task of standing by in case of accidents during this novel and tricky manoeuvre was done. The three lighthouse keepers had just unwittingly witnessed a truly historic moment: the first joint mission of lifeboat and helicopter. In the ensuing decades this combination would advance the business of saving life at sea as comprehensively as had the development of the motor lifeboat in the period covered by this book.

There is one other intriguing detail to be added to the story of this pioneering mission. The young man who flew the Westland WS 51 Dragonfly helicopter out to the Wolf Rock that day was one Alan Bristow, chief test pilot for Westland Aircraft Ltd. Five years later he would go on to found the world-renowned Bristow Helicopters, the company which, among its many other operations, provides the crew and aircraft for today's Maritime and Coastguard Agency search and rescue service.

It was a week later when the three men on the lighthouse were finally relieved from their long watch. A celebratory Cornish pasty had been baked for them of such a size that while one end rested in the oven, the other needed to be propped on a chair. When asked how they spent their long days and nights, they replied, 'playing the gramophone and arguing'. Their last argument had been on Darwin's theory of evolution and the record they played over and over again was one called *Solitude*.

Bibliography

PRIMARY SOURCES

British Library, Newspaper Library – various contemporary local newspapers
The Graham Farr Archives
Royal National Lifeboat Institution Archives

SECONDARY SOURCES

Burg, Amos, Autobiographical notes
Cameron, Ian, *Riders of the Storm,* London, Weidenfeld & Nicolson, 2002
Cockcroft, Barry, *Fatal Call of the Running Tide,* London, Hodder & Stoughton, 1995
Cox, Barry, *Lifeboat Gallantry,* London, Spink & Son, 1998
Denton, Tony, *Lifeboat Enthusiasts' Society Handbook 2003*
Farr, Graham, *Wreck and Rescue in the Bristol Channel* (1 and 2), D. Bradford Barton Ltd, 1966–7
——, *Wreck and Rescue on the Coast of Devon*, D. Bradford Barton Ltd, 1968
Howarth, Patrick, *Lifeboat: In Danger's Hour,* London, Hamlyn, 1981
Morris, Jeff, Various 'Station Histories'
Noall, Cyril and Farr, Graham, *Wreck and Rescue round the Cornish Coast* (1, 2 and 3), D. Bradford Barton Ltd, 1964–5
Royal National Lifeboat Institution, *The Lifeboat* journal and Annual Reports
Vince, Charles, *Storm on the Waters,* London, Hodder & Stoughton, 1946

Index